Elevating Your Professional Effectiveness
and Personal Wellbeing

Further Faster

20 Life Principles to Achieve More and Avoid Burnout

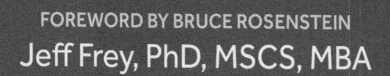

FOREWORD BY BRUCE ROSENSTEIN

Jeff Frey, PhD, MSCS, MBA

Copyright © 2025, Jeff Frey, PhD.

All rights reserved.

No part of this book may be reproduced or transmitted in any form or by any means, electronic or mechanical, including photocopying, recording, or by any information retrieval system, without permission in writing from the publisher.

Publishing Process by www.PlugAndPlayPublishing.com

Book Cover by Tracey Miller | www.TraceOfStyle.com

Book Edited by Jenny Butterfield Lyon and Nicole Marron

Disclaimer: This book contains opinions, ideas, experiences, and exercises. The purchaser and/or reader of these materials assumes all responsibility for the use of this information. Jeff Frey and Publisher assume no responsibility and/or liability whatsoever for any purchaser and/or reader of these materials.

To Wesley: As you turn thirteen, I pass down the lessons I've learned from my father, mentors, teachers, researchers, and guides who have shaped these principles. May you grow with wisdom, resilience, and purpose. This is for you and for all those who choose to follow.

Praise for FurtherFaster

"Paradox is a confusing but ever-present aspect of life. In this book, Frey offers a series of paradoxes shouting for reflection and action. The latest research could easily reverse which option is 'further' and which is 'faster'—both work and are worthy aspirations for a more fulfilling and effective life."

— **Richard E. Boyatzis**
Distinguished University Professor, Case Western Reserve University
and author of *The Science of Change*

"Jeff's *FurtherFaster* delivers timeless lessons for anyone chasing big goals amidst real-life demands. Whether you're an athlete, educator, or entrepreneur, you'll find principles that resonate and inspire, launching you to the next level."

— **Becky Wade Firth**
Author of *Run the World*
Four-time U.S. Olympic Trials Participant
High School Cross-Country Coach

"*FurtherFaster* is not at all what I expected it to be. As an avid consumer of treatises on personal and professional development, I assumed this would be yet another indictment of my failure to keep the pace, roaring ahead down the road to success. What a delightful surprise to discover that author Jeff Frey has provided a compendium of counterintuitive concepts designed to challenge our thinking about the way we live today. The yin-yang principles articulated in each chapter are supported by thoughtful assessments to measure readers' current state of being, followed by a set of practical suggestions that are actionable rather than intimidating. Contradictory ideas such as 'save some money' and 'spend some money'—sprinkled throughout the book—demand readers' attention. The principles behind each opposing notion, supported by research and accompanied by personal anecdotes, represent a framework (not a formula) for reinvention. *FurtherFaster* is just the kind of whole-life manual that our upside-down world demands."

— **Ronnie Hagerty Ph.D., CFRE**
Assistant Vice President, United Way of Greater Houston

"*FurtherFaster* speaks to the essential role of innovation—not just in business but across all facets of life. Jeff's work is a reminder that when leaders get stuck trying to bring their companies to the next level, they can break through those business barriers by tackling personal blind spots. His framework is a practical guide to making meaningful progress in life that unlocks leadership potential for business growth."

— **Andrea Kates**
Former Tech CEO
Author of *From Stuck to Scale*

"Jeff Frey's *FurtherFaster* is a practical guide to a daily mindset that will position you for personal fulfillment while having a positive impact on others. If you practice these principles, not only will your life change for the better, but people's lives will be transformed through you. This book is a must-read for anyone looking to live and lead with integrity and purpose."

— **Kent Chevalier**
Pittsburgh Steelers Chaplain
Athletes in Action

"*FurtherFaster* delivers a unique framework for those who want to excel. Dr. Frey draws from academic research and professional case studies to offer practical principles that resonate deeply with leaders navigating complex challenges in business and life. Its insights are especially valuable at pivotal moments, offering a roadmap to achieve sustainable growth and impact."

— **Dr. Varun Nagaraj**
Dean, S.P. Jain Institute of Management & Research, Mumbai, India

Take Your Life to the Next Level with the FREE FurtherFaster Assessment!

Inside every chapter in this book, you'll have the opportunity to self-assess and reflect. But what if you could quickly and easily answer the same questions and get a completely customized report with recommendations just for you?

If so, let me introduce you to...

The FurtherFaster Assessment (FREE for Readers of This Book!)

In less than 10 minutes, you'll not only receive a deeper insight into the ten areas we discuss in this book, but you'll also get a custom plan tailored to your unique scores so you can...

- Create quick wins and build momentum in your life
- Boost your progress toward your goals
- Achieve sustainable, long-term growth
- And much, much more!

How It Works

1. Visit www.FurtherFaster.com/bookoffer.

2. Enter this exclusive promo code to unlock the full assessment: **FURTHERFASTER2025**.

3. Answer the questions to instantly get your custom report and recommendations.

There's no better time to act than right now! Take the free assessment, unlock the insights you need, and start your journey to moving FurtherFaster!

Acknowledgments

This book would not have been possible without the unwavering support of my family—my wife, Stephanie, and our two boys, Wesley and Colton—who gave me the time and space to bring these ideas to life.

I'm deeply grateful to my pivotal educators, especially Al Napier and Richard Boyatzis, whose guidance shaped much of my thinking.

And I'm grateful to Weston Lyon and Jenny Butterfield Lyon for their indispensable help in the writing process.

Special thanks to Kris, Debbie, Randy, Rosemarie, Abigail, Nikki, Glenn, Ben, and Sonya for their thoughtful feedback.

Finally, thank you to the early adopters of the FurtherFaster Principles and my students, clients, followers, and readers, whose engagement and insights were instrumental in refining these ideas. This book is for you as much as it is for the future generations who choose to follow.

Table of Contents

Foreword 1

Read This First 5

Section 1 - Emotional Wellbeing 11

Further Principle - Empathize with Others 15

Faster Principle - Motivate from Within 21

Go FurtherFaster in Your 27
Emotional Wellbeing

Section 2 - Environmental Wellbeing 29

Further Principle - Give Things Away 33

Faster Principle - Find Selfish Space 39

Go FurtherFaster in Your 47
Environmental Wellbeing

Section 3 - Financial Wellbeing 49

Further Principle - Save Some Money 51

Faster Principle - Spend Some Money 57

Go FurtherFaster in Your 63
Financial Wellbeing

Section 4 - Intellectual Wellbeing 65

Further Principle - Understand Basic Things 67

Faster Principle - Disrupt Traditional Methods 73

Go FurtherFaster in Your 79
  Intellectual Wellbeing

Section 5 - Organizational Wellbeing **81**

Further Principle - Remain Highly Adaptable 85

Faster Principle - Waste No Time 91

Go FurtherFaster in Your 97
Organizational Wellbeing

Section 6 - Physical Wellbeing **99**

Further Principle - Just Stay Still 101

Faster Principle - Just Keep Moving 107

Go FurtherFaster in Your 115
Physical Wellbeing

Section 7 - Recreational Wellbeing **117**

Further Principle - Finish Something Hard 119

Faster Principle - Make It Easy 125

Go FurtherFaster in Your 131
Recreational Wellbeing

Section 8 - Relational Wellbeing **133**

Further Principle - Love Your People 135

Faster Principle - Find New Friends 141

Go FurtherFaster in Your 149
Relational Wellbeing

Section 9 - Spiritual Wellbeing **151**

Further Principle - Listen to Truth 153

Faster Principle - Learn with Purpose 159

Go FurtherFaster in Your 165
Spiritual Wellbeing

Section 10 - Vocational Wellbeing **167**

Further Principle - Become an Expert 171

Faster Principle - Do Many Things 177

Go FurtherFaster in Your 183
Vocational Wellbeing

Next Steps - Your Journey Begins Here 185

Take Your Life to the Next Level with the 189
FREE FurtherFaster Assessment!

About the Author 191

Looking for a Dynamic Speaker to Elevate 193
Your Next Event?

Motivate and Inspire Others! 197

Works Cited 199

Foreword

In 2009, I published *Living in More Than One World*, a book born out of a desire to help people live richer, more fulfilling lives by embracing the full spectrum of their talents, passions, and responsibilities. At its heart, the book was a call to action—a reminder that we are at our best when we live integrated lives, where personal growth, professional achievement, and meaningful relationships coexist and amplify one another.

Shortly after the book's release, I received a message from Jeff Frey. He shared how *Living in More Than One World* resonated with him and gave voice to ideas he had already been exploring in his own life. His enthusiasm and insights stood out to me immediately. Here was someone who not only understood the concepts but embodied those concepts in profound ways. Over the years, Jeff and I stayed in touch, and I had the privilege of watching his journey unfold—a journey that reflects the spirit of living in more than one world and now culminates in the principles of *FurtherFaster*.

Jeff's story is a powerful one. With a career that spans technology, academia, and leadership, he exemplifies what it means to weave together diverse threads into a cohesive and meaningful life. As a leader, educator, innovator, and father, Jeff has embraced the challenges and rewards of operating across multiple domains. He has done so with the conviction that success is not about sacrificing one part of life for another but about creating a sustainable rhythm that honors our ambitions, responsibilities, and personal well-being.

FurtherFaster builds on this philosophy in compelling and actionable ways. At its core, the book is about navigating the tension between achievement and sustainability—a challenge that defines modern life. Jeff brings a deeply personal perspective to this topic, informed by his own experiences and by years of research in emotional intelligence, leadership, and resilience.

What I admire most about *FurtherFaster* is its dual focus. On one hand, it offers practical strategies for excelling in our professional lives—guiding us to be more effective, innovative, and results-driven. On the other, it underscores the importance of renewal, self-care, and long-term thinking. These principles are not presented as opposites but as complementary forces that, when balanced, enable us to thrive.

As I reflect on my own work, I see clear parallels between the ideas Jeff presents in *FurtherFaster* and the core tenets of *Living in More Than One World*. Both books challenge the notion that life must be compartmentalized into rigid silos. Both advocate for a more holistic approach, where our personal and professional pursuits inform and enrich one another. And both recognize that true fulfillment comes not from chasing a single goal but from cultivating a life of purpose, connection, and continual growth.

One of the aspects of *FurtherFaster* that particularly resonates with me is its emphasis on the "how." Jeff doesn't just describe the principles; he provides actionable steps that readers can apply to their own lives. From setting boundaries to nurturing relationships, from building resilience to fostering innovation, the book equips readers with the tools they need to navigate complexity with clarity and confidence.

In my own work, I've often spoken about the importance of intentionality—of making deliberate choices that align with our values and aspirations. Jeff's book takes this idea a step further, showing how we can integrate intentionality into every aspect of our lives, from the smallest daily habits to the biggest career decisions.

I also want to highlight the deeply human element of *FurtherFaster*. This is not a book of abstract theories or unattainable ideals. It is rooted in real-world experiences and challenges, inside and outside the workplace. Jeff's insights are grounded in authenticity and empathy, making them accessible and relatable to readers from all walks of life.

I want to express my gratitude to Jeff for inviting me to contribute to this book. It is a privilege to see how the ideas I've shared over the years have influenced and intersected with his journey. It is even more rewarding to see how Jeff has taken these ideas, expanded upon them, and made them his own.

FurtherFaster is a testament to the power of living a multidimensional life. It is a call to action for anyone who wants to achieve more without losing sight of what matters most. And it is a reminder that true success is not about doing everything at once, but about doing the right things at the right time with purpose and intention.

I encourage you to approach this book with an open mind and a willingness to reflect. Let it inspire you to think differently, to act boldly, and to live fully. As you turn the pages, may you discover not only strategies for success but also a deeper sense of what it means to thrive in today's fast-paced world.

– Bruce Rosenstein
Managing Editor, *Leader to Leader*
Author, *Living in More Than One World: How Peter Drucker's Wisdom Can Inspire and Transform Your Life* and *Create Your Future the Peter Drucker Way: Developing and Applying a Forward-Focused Mindset*

Read This First

Somewhere around the end of middle school, I started hearing a familiar pattern, "Get good grades, play a sport, join the student council, and more." When I asked "Why?" the answer was to get into a good high school. When I asked "Why?" again in high school, the answer was to get into a good college. Then, when I asked "Why?" in college, the answer was to get a good job. And so on. Every goal I was told to pursue now was tied to achieving something later on, always pushing further ahead faster.

That's when the idea of **FurtherFaster** was born, and I started using the concept to pick the next right path for my goals. In fact, I used the concept so much that my parents even made me shirts and embroidered hats with the phrase to support my ambitions.

Since then, the concept has shown up everywhere in my life—a youth group I led, a band I started, a course I taught in college, and finally, the culmination of my PhD studies.

Over the past three decades of working with students, clients, and corporations, I've honed these principles and seen them help people make meaningful changes in their lives.

But What Exactly Does FurtherFaster Mean?

At its core, FurtherFaster is **both a mindset and a way of living**, prioritizing two seemingly opposite forces:

- **Further** is about personal wellbeing, sustainability, and longevity.

- **Faster** is about professional effectiveness, quick wins, and measurable achievements.

Focusing only on long-term sustainability (Further) may leave you waiting to achieve anything significant today. Chasing only short-term achievements (Faster) can leave you burned out and empty.

The point isn't to choose between the two—it's to hold both in harmony, like yin and yang. This philosophy is not just about achieving more or moving quickly; it's about learning how to prioritize both your lasting wellbeing and your immediate wins. There is a natural push and pull, an interdependence of these two opposing forces in life, that this book brings to your attention. These forces don't contradict each other. But rather, when done well, they exist in harmony.

A New Way of Living, Not a Trend

This book is not a quick-win recipe or how-to guide for specific areas of life. It's also not a "go-go-go" manifesto encouraging you to live at breakneck speed without pause.

In fact, if you approach this book expecting to find only life hacks or productivity tips, you'll miss the bigger picture. This book challenges the very notion of speed for speed's sake.

This is not just a trendy book on how to get ahead.

Instead, this book is a **whole-life strategy manual**. The combination of the FurtherFaster Principles is designed to serve as a "yellow light" that encourages you to look at your daily life and make decisions that serve both today's goals and tomorrow's wellbeing.

This book is about developing a mindset where both **personal wellbeing and professional effectiveness** are important, not sacrificing one for the other. It's about learning to navigate life intentionally—understanding that there are times to push forward at full speed and times to ease off the gas.

As you learn about the FurtherFaster Principles, I encourage you to use the principles and tools in each chapter to **assess your current state**, **identify strengths and growth opportunities**, and **take action with purpose**.

Whether you're looking to enhance your relationships, improve your financial health, or find more joy in recreational activities, this book gives you the roadmap to make conscious choices about moving forward in life.

Your Roadmap to Go FurtherFaster

There are ten sections in this book, each representing a core dimension of wellbeing:

- Emotional
- Environmental
- Financial
- Intellectual
- Organizational
- Physical
- Recreational
- Relational
- Spiritual
- Vocational

These sections are not organized in a way that requires you to read this book from front to back. Instead, each section contains practical strategies to help you assess where you are, where you want to go, and how to move Further and Faster.

You can read any section that speaks to you, assess your strengths and growth areas, and jump-start your journey toward greater wellbeing in that area.

Within each section, I introduce **Further and Faster principles**—one focusing on **sustainability and longevity (Further)** and the other on **effectiveness and quick wins (Faster)**. These principles are like two sides of the same coin. Whichever section you choose to start with, please read both chapters in that section to get a complete picture of how to use the information to your greatest benefit.

Each chapter also includes assessments and activities to help you gain greater insight into the principle. Don't feel the need to complete all the activities. As with the sections in this book, choose the activities that most speak to you to start making gains in your life.

Ready to Move FurtherFaster?

If you're ready to dive in and take your next steps toward a **whole-life transformation**, this book is your guide—harmonizing the necessities of long-term wellbeing with immediate results.

Let's get started!

Section 1
Emotional Wellbeing

Emotional Wellbeing refers to the emotional quality of an individual's life. It encompasses the ability to generate positive emotions, moods, thoughts, and feelings even in the face of stressful experiences or adverse psychological, economic, or situational factors. According to Fredrickson's Broaden-and-Build Theory of Positive Emotions, cultivating positive emotions broadens our ability to think creatively and build lasting psychological resources over time [1].

This makes Emotional Wellbeing a cornerstone of overall health and wellness, impacting your mental state and your long-term success in all areas of life. As the first section of this book, Emotional Wellbeing lays the groundwork for everything that follows. Mastering your emotions will strengthen your ability to succeed personally and professionally, encouraging growth in all other dimensions of wellness.

The Further and Faster principles outlined here will help you enhance your Emotional Wellbeing by focusing on two key aspects: empathy and internal motivation. Let's explore how these principles can enhance your emotional health and overall wellbeing.

To Go Further: Empathize with Others

Empathy allows you to go further by building strong relationships and support networks that sustain you. When you empathize with others, you not only do something good for them, but they feel endeared to you. This network of supportive individuals with whom you have been empathetic over time can take you further in life. Without empathy, you risk alienating people and making enemies, leading to conflict and isolation. Stepping on or over others for short-term gain may have immediate benefits, but these are fleeting and often have significant negative consequences.

To Go Faster: Motivate from Within

Internal motivation, on the other hand, propels you to go faster by pushing you toward your goals with self-driven energy. Motivating from within means you don't rely on external sources to get ahead. Your actions shape your destiny, allowing you to make things happen on your terms. Without this internal motivation, you depend on people, money, jobs, social validation, status, recognition, and rewards. When these external sources fail you, progress halts, and you can't move at all, let alone go faster toward your goals.

They may seem like opposing forces, but focusing solely on empathy might leave you dependent on others, while relying only on self-motivation can lead to personal burnout.

Now, let's take a closer look at each principle and discover how embracing empathy and cultivating intrinsic motivation can enhance your Emotional Wellbeing.

Further Principle

Empathize with Others

"Empathy is patiently and sincerely seeing the world through the other person's eyes. It is not learned in school; it is cultivated over a lifetime."

- Albert Einstein

Empathy is the ability to step into another person's shoes, to see and feel the world as they do. Going deeper means understanding another person's thoughts, emotions, and actions from their perspective. When you embody empathy, you connect with others emotionally, recognizing their experiences and validating their feelings.

Empathic individuals respond with compassion and understanding, offering support and comfort without judgment. This involves a willingness to be vulnerable, to open yourself up to another's pain or joy. When you practice empathy, you build trust, deepen connections, and help to create a supportive network to sustain you in both good and challenging times, strengthening the fabric of our communities.

In the workplace, empathetic leaders are more effective at motivating and inspiring their teams because they can better understand the needs and perspectives of their team members. In fact, a new study by Catalyst found that when employees perceive their leaders as empathetic, they are more likely to be engaged and innovative and less likely to leave the organization [2].

Beyond the workplace, empathy allows us to build deeper connections with others, navigate social situations more effectively, and be more attuned to the needs of those around us. Empathy is a key predictor of success in our personal lives, as research has shown that people with higher levels of empathy who can regulate their emotions tend to have more satisfying romantic relationships, stronger social support networks, and better mental health outcomes [3].

As you can see, the research suggests that developing empathy can be a powerful tool for achieving greater success and fulfillment in *all* areas of our lives—including becoming more effective leaders, more valued team members, and more compassionate and successful individuals overall.

Empathy in My Son

From an early age, my son has shown an interesting sign of high empathy when watching movies or TV shows. During suspenseful moments where a character is doing something they shouldn't and is on the verge of getting caught (like searching the coach's office as footsteps are heading down the hall), my son plugs his ears, covers his eyes, or hides under a blanket. It's not the explosions or the scary action scenes that get to him but the thought of someone being embarrassed or uncomfortable.

But empathy is more than just feeling for others; it's about understanding their emotions and possibly even sharing their experiences. When my son covers his eyes, he's not just reacting to the tension; he's placing himself in the character's shoes, feeling their anxiety and dread. He feels like he will get caught; he knows what that feels like and doesn't like it. He wants to avoid the feeling of that situation himself.

Seeing this in my son reminds me of the importance of nurturing empathy in myself and those around me. The trick when we're adults is to let ourselves feel that emotion and then take action with or for that person. This level of empathetic action-taking is a powerful tool for navigating the complexities of human interactions and creating meaningful connections.

Empathy is a trait that can transform our personal and professional relationships, making us better friends, colleagues, and leaders.

Developing Deeper Empathy

Empathy is one of those things that makes us uniquely human—the ability to truly understand and share another person's feelings. Yet, in our busy lives, it's easy to overlook or underestimate the power of empathy. Developing empathy can lead to so many benefits in life, but first, we need to assess where we stand.

Ask yourself the following questions and rate yourself from 0 to 5, with 0 being "Never," 1 "Rarely," 2 "Sometimes," 3 "Often," 4 "Usually," and 5 "Always":

_____ I express my emotions in ways that are not offensive to others.

_____ I come into contact with new people regularly.

_____ I listen more than I talk when meeting someone new.

_____ I take action to help others when I sense they are struggling.

_____ I recognize and interpret nonverbal cues from others accurately.

_____ **TOTAL**

Now, take all your numbers and add them up to get your total score. For example, if you rated yourself a four in every area, your total score would be 20. Here's how to interpret your results:

- 21 - 25: Bravo! You have a high level of empathy. Keep nurturing this skill to enhance your personal and professional relationships.

- 16 - 20: You're doing pretty well, but there's room for improvement. Consider focusing on areas where you scored lower to enhance your empathetic abilities.

- 15 or below: Don't worry. Check out the activities below to learn how to increase your score.

No matter your score—though some people, like my son, are just born with a high level of empathy—it has been clinically proven that empathy is a skill that can be developed over time with practice and intention. Here are some practical activities you can engage in to enhance your empathy:

Active Listening Exercise: Spend 15 minutes conversing with someone and practicing active listening. Focus on their words, repeat back to them what they've said in your own words, and then ask how they feel about it. You may find you are spot on or a little off. This practice can help you become more attuned to others' emotions.

Body Language Study: Take some time to learn about body language. Read books or watch videos on nonverbal communication and observe people around you. See if you can interpret their body language and emotional states. My wife and I play this game with my sons in the airport, mall, or park: "How do you think that person feels right now?"

Empathy Through Media: Engage with stories in books, movies, or TV shows that explore diverse experiences. Put yourself in the character's shoes and think about how you would feel in their situations. Let yourself feel what they feel—get mad, laugh, and cry with them. If this is tough for you, take someone with high empathy to a movie and tuning into their emotions instead of those on screen.

By actively practicing these activities, you will become more empathetic, understanding, and connected to the people around you.

Faster Principle

Motivate from Within

"What lies behind us and what lies before us are tiny matters compared to what lies within us."

- Ralph Waldo Emerson

Motivating from within means finding the drive to pursue goals and tasks from an internal source rather than relying on external rewards or pressures. Personal passions, values, and a sense of purpose fuel this intrinsic motivation. Engaging in activities that fulfill you and resonate with your core beliefs is at the heart of this principle.

Focusing on external motivations, on the other hand, like rewards or recognition, can leave you with fleeting inspiration. Those external rewards might push you forward temporarily, but they lack the staying power of internal motivation.

To illustrate this point, studies published in 2017 by the *Journal of Personality and Social Psychology* and *Frontiers in Human Neuroscience* found that people who were intrinsically motivated to pursue their goals (i.e., driven by personal interests and values) experienced greater wellbeing and were more likely to accomplish their objectives compared to those who were extrinsically motivated (driven by external rewards or pressures). The researchers concluded that the more intrinsically motivated individuals are, the more likely they are to attain their goals and the more positive consequences they experience as a result [4] [5].

As for intrinsic motivation in the workplace, research published in the Harvard Business Review in 2019 examined the factors that contribute to long-term employee engagement and performance. The study revealed that workers motivated by a strong sense of purpose and personal fulfillment (intrinsic motivation) consistently outperformed those primarily driven by external rewards or incentives. The authors emphasized that "fostering intrinsic motivation should be a top priority for leaders who want to build high-performing, sustainable organizations" [6].

As the research has shown, self-driven people constantly seek personal growth through their pursuits, finding joy and satisfaction in the process of a job well done.

Do It Well

My dad used to tell me, "If you're going to do anything, do it well."

The idea is simple: Whatever task you undertake, give it your all. Even if there's no external recognition or reward, the satisfaction of knowing you did your best should be enough.

While I have some not-so-fond memories of how this mantra applied to anything and absolutely everything—from washing dishes to taking college exams to running marathons—I'm glad he passed this idea on to me. It has become invaluable. It's become a driver at home, at work, at school, with family and friends, and in everything I do.

Sometimes, people around me think I'm out to be the best to one-up them. Whether working on a small project or a major career milestone, I always strive to find that inner drive to excel. But it's not about the competition or the accolades; it's about personal integrity and pushing myself to reach my full potential. This internal motivation has helped me achieve goals and overcome challenges I would have never thought possible, providing me with a deep sense of fulfillment and purpose.

When summing up passages from Aristotle, Will Durant wrote, "We are what we repeatedly do. Excellence, then, is not an act, but a habit." I urge those of you who are reading this to make excellence a habit in your life. I've seen firsthand how powerful intrinsic motivation can be. It keeps you going when the going gets tough, helps you rise above obstacles, and pushes you to achieve great things.

Mastering Internal Motivation

Finding motivation from within is one of the most powerful drivers for achieving your goals and living a fulfilling life. It's not about the external rewards or recognitions; it's about the passion and purpose that fuels you from the inside. But first, we need to assess where we stand.

Ask yourself the following questions and rate yourself from 0 to 5, with 0 being "Never," 1 "Rarely," 2 "Sometimes," 3 "Often," 4 "Usually," and 5 "Always":

_____ I experience internal motivation stronger than external.

_____ I set realistic expectations for myself.

_____ I say "no" without feeling guilty.

_____ I understand my passion and purpose.

_____ I have a talent, skill, or activity I continue to master

_____ **TOTAL**

Now, take all your numbers and add them up to get your total score. For example, if you rated yourself a four in every area, your total score would be 20. Here's how to interpret your results:

- 21 - 25: Great! You have a high level of internal motivation. Keep nurturing this intrinsic drive to maintain and enhance your personal and professional success.

- 16 - 20: You're doing pretty well, but there's room for improvement. To enhance your internal motivation, consider focusing on areas where you scored lower.

- 15 or below: Don't worry. Look at some activities below to learn how to increase your score.

No matter your score, we can all stoke the fire of our inner motivation from time to time. Here are some practical activities you can engage in to foster your internal drive:

Passion Journal: Start a journal dedicated to your passions and interests. Write down what you love to do, why you love it, and how it makes you feel. Reflect on how these activities align with your values and goals and how you might bring some of your other, *not*-so-motivated tasks into closer alignment with them.

Set Personal Goals: Identify a personal goal that you may need to be more motivated to accomplish. Break it into smaller, manageable tasks tied to an activity you may be motivated to do. Then, set a timeline for achieving each. Track your progress and celebrate small victories along the way. Give yourself permission to sprinkle in some external motivation during these celebration times.

Daily Reflection: For a solid week, spend 5 to 10 minutes at the end of each day reflecting on what motivated you during the day. Consider what activities or interactions gave you energy and how you can incorporate more of those into your life.

Focusing on what truly drives you can cultivate a deeper sense of motivation, even for the things you aren't motivated to do at first.

Go FurtherFaster in Your Emotional Wellbeing

Emotional Wellbeing is a cornerstone of overall health and happiness, encompassing our ability to connect with others and find inner drive. In this section, we explored two vital principles: Empathize with Others and Motivate from Within.

Empathize with Others: This principle encourages you to deeply connect with those around you, promoting trust, understanding, and strong relationships. Empathy is more than just a moral virtue; it is a powerful skill that can transform your personal and professional life, helping you build a supportive network and easily navigate complex social dynamics [7].

Motivate from Within: This principle shifts the focus inward, highlighting the power of intrinsic motivation. You can achieve sustained success and personal fulfillment by cultivating an internal drive rooted in your passions and values. Valuing intrinsic motivation teaches you to find your energy from within, enabling you to push toward your goals with purpose and resilience, even when external rewards are lacking.

By embracing both empathy and intrinsic motivation, you cultivate a resilient emotional foundation that allows you to thrive in every aspect of life. Prioritizing each principle enhances your personal growth and positions you to make a meaningful impact on those around you. Use these principles to go FurtherFaster in your pursuit of emotional health and wellbeing, knowing that a well-rounded emotional life is key to a fulfilling and prosperous existence.

Section 2
Environmental Wellbeing

Environmental Wellbeing refers to the quality of a person's surroundings and their ability to maintain good health by creating comfortable, stimulating, equitable, and safe spaces—both public and private. This aspect of wellbeing goes beyond just the physical environment; it also supports our mental and emotional state. As Evans and McCoy demonstrated in their research, poorly designed environments can negatively impact human health, while well-maintained, thoughtful spaces contribute to mental clarity, emotional health, and physical wellbeing [8].

A well-curated environment enhances our overall quality of life, contributing to a sense of peace and belonging. Let's explore the Further and Faster principles to enhance Environmental Wellbeing and understand how shaping the spaces around us—both external and internal—can lead to improved health and wellbeing.

To Go Further: Give Things Away

Giving things away helps create a clutter-free, peaceful environment and encourages a mindset of abundance and sharing. You need to cultivate this habit to avoid overwhelming yourself with unnecessary possessions, which can lead to stress and a feeling of being trapped by material goods. In addition, helping others fosters a sense of community and goodwill and encourages others to care for you in return. You need to practice generosity to avoid becoming isolated, materialistic, and disconnected from the community around you.

To Go Faster: Find Selfish Space

Finding selfish space allows you to recharge and maintain your health, providing immediate relief and focus. Taking "me time" ensures you have the energy and mental clarity to achieve your goals. If you neglect this, you risk burnout and a constant sense of being overwhelmed, which can negatively impact your personal and professional life. Prioritizing your needs and ensuring you have a dedicated space to relax and rejuvenate enables you to approach your tasks with renewed vigor and efficiency.

To connect deeply with the world around us, we must recognize that we are part of a whole. Prioritizing generosity for others (the whole) while also carving out personal space (the part) ensures a healthy environment around us both for the future and in the here and now. Giving things away promotes long-term sustainability, while finding selfish space provides immediate gains.

Let's talk deeper about each principle to understand how giving things away and finding selfish space can help you build a sustainable and fulfilling environment.

Further Principle

Give Things Away

"We know only well that what we are doing is nothing more than a drop in the ocean. But if the drop were not there, the ocean would be missing something."

- Mother Teresa

Giving things away extends far beyond the simple act of donating material possessions; it's about sharing your time, energy, and skills to benefit others and foster a sense of community. Individuals who embrace this principle are driven by a spirit of generosity and selflessness, actively seeking opportunities to make a positive impact on those around them.

Research underscores the profound benefits of this practice. A study by the University of Hong Kong found that people who volunteer their time and resources experience a marked increase in life satisfaction compared to those who do not volunteer [9]. This boost in happiness is attributed to the deep sense of fulfillment derived from knowing they are making a difference, whether through small acts of kindness or more significant contributions of time, talent, or treasure. The generosity of giving creates a ripple effect, cultivating a culture of gratitude and mutual support.

Moreover, the act of giving also enhances personal growth and development. A study by the Corporation for National and Community Service found that regular volunteers have a 27% higher likelihood of finding employment compared to non-volunteers [10]. This can be attributed to the valuable networking opportunities, the acquisition of new skills, and the demonstration of a proactive attitude and sense of responsibility. In this way, giving things away is not only an altruistic act but also a strategy that can yield tangible benefits, including improved job prospects and professional growth.

The Cycle of Generosity

My dad had a saying: "If God can get it through you, God will get it to you." This wasn't about prosperity or a transactional mindset; it was a genuine belief in the transformative power of generosity. Growing up, I witnessed him live out this principle daily. The more he gave—whether it was his time, money, or talents—the more he seemed to receive. But the gifts he received weren't meant to be hoarded; they were meant to be shared even further.

My dad's philosophy also aligns perfectly with the idea that true wealth comes from what we share with others, not what we keep for ourselves. And his example illustrates how living generously can create a cycle of abundance that benefits everyone.

For example, I started a mentoring program for college students a few years ago, pairing them with accomplished C-level executives. To my surprise, the mentors expressed more gratitude than the mentees as they found immense joy and fulfillment in giving their time and sharing their wisdom.

Research supports this, too: Mentors often gain more from the relationship than those they mentor. Why? Because sharing our knowledge and experiences enriches others while deepening our understanding and giving us renewed purpose [11].

The act of giving truly enriches both the receiver and the giver. The more we give, the more we grow, and the more we find to give. This cycle of generosity strengthens our communities and creates a more connected, compassionate world.

Actions for a More Generous Life

Giving is one of the most enriching experiences you can have. It's not just about helping others; it's about creating a ripple effect of kindness and generosity that can transform lives, including your own. By giving things away—whether it's material possessions, time, or skills—you also create emotional and psychological benefits for yourself. Decluttering your physical space, for example, often leads to a decluttering of the mind [12]. And the act of donating items or sharing resources grows a sense of accomplishment, reduces stress, and promotes a feeling of abundance rather than scarcity.

Additionally, giving can be a deeply empowering act. It allows you to assert agency over your possessions and resources, deciding actively to contribute to the wellbeing of others. This intentional act of giving can improve your self-esteem and mental health, making you feel more connected to your community and more aligned with your personal values. It's a reminder that you have the power to make a difference, not just in your life but in the lives of those around you.

Ask yourself the following questions and rate yourself from 0 to 5, with 0 being "Never," 1 "Rarely," 2 "Sometimes," 3 "Often," 4 "Usually," and 5 "Always":

_____ I do something when I see a safety hazard or people and animals in trouble.

_____ I regularly give away items or resources that I no longer need to benefit others.

_____ I engage in at least one activity a year that contributes to the environment.

_____ I participate actively in a civic club or a community service organization.

_____ I give time to at least one organization that helps my community.

_____ **TOTAL**

Now, take all your numbers and add them up to get your total score. For example, if you rated yourself a four in every area, your total score would be 20. Here's how to interpret your results:

- 21 - 25: Awesome! You are highly engaged in giving back to others and your community. Keep nurturing this generous spirit.

- 16 - 20: You're doing pretty well, but there's room for improvement. Consider focusing on areas where you scored lower to enhance your giving habits.

- 15 or below: This isn't a problem. You can start giving any time.

No matter your score, giving is a skill that can be developed and integrated into your daily life with practice and intention. Here are some practical steps to help you embrace the joy of giving:

Volunteer: Find a local organization that aligns with your interests and commit to volunteering there at least once a month. Your time can significantly impact their operations, whether it's a food bank, animal shelter, or community center.

Random Acts of Kindness: Make it a habit to perform one small, selfless act each day. This could be holding the door open for someone, giving a compliment, or donating to a cause. As you do them, notice how these small actions make you feel and the impact they have on others.

Resource Sharing: Identify items you no longer need and donate them to those who can use them. This can include clothes, books, food, money, your time, skills, expertise, blood donations, volunteer work, or even simple handwritten notes or handmade crafts.

By integrating these practices into your life, you can create a sense of abundance in your life while creating a better overall environment for all.

Faster Principle

Find Selfish Space

"Please put your mask on first before helping others."
- Every Flight Attendant Ever

Finding selfish space involves intentionally setting aside time and creating a mental environment that focuses solely on your needs and wellbeing. It's about recognizing the value of self-care and prioritizing your mental, emotional, and physical health. This can be achieved through practices that promote clarity and mastery, such as mindfulness, meditation, or simply enjoying a quiet moment alone.

However, let's pause to consider the word "selfish." In our society, this term often carries a negative connotation, suggesting a lack of concern for others. But what if we reclaimed "selfish" to mean something essential and positive? In this context, being "selfish" doesn't mean neglecting others or being self-centered; instead, it refers to the necessary act of self-preservation and prioritizing our wellbeing. Think of it as filling your own cup first so you have more to give to others, understanding that by taking care of yourself, you can better serve those around you. Reclaiming the word "selfish" in this way helps us see that prioritizing our own health and needs isn't just okay; it's important for sustainable wellbeing and effective contribution to our communities.

People who embody this principle understand the necessity of establishing boundaries and moments of solitude to recharge. They know the importance of disconnecting from external pressures and distractions to reconnect with themselves.

This also means knowing when to say "no." It's important to recognize that it's okay to decline requests or set limits when others ask for your time or energy in ways that compromise your own needs. Saying "no" is not about being unkind or selfish in a negative sense; it's about protecting your wellbeing so that you can be your best self. Learning to say "no" when necessary is a powerful act of self-care, ensuring that your own resources are not depleted to the point where you have nothing left to give.

And this isn't just at home. Finding selfish space in the workplace is another area where it proves essential. A 2020 survey revealed that 76% of employees experience burnout on the job at least sometimes, and 28% say they are burned out "very often" or "always" at work. This feeling is largely due to insufficient personal time compared to work demands. Those who managed to carve out regular "me time" experienced significantly lower levels of burnout, underscoring the critical role of personal time in maintaining mental health [13].

Phil Knight, the co-founder of Nike, also emphasizes this concept in his book *Shoe Dog*, where he discusses the importance of finding "selfish space" amid the pressures of building a business: "The only way to do it is to do it. Meaning you have to make the time. You have to make space in your life. You have to carve it out. No one else is going to do it for you" [14].

Taking time for oneself is a critical component of overall wellbeing and in living an effective, fulfilling life at home and work.

The Power of Selfish Space

At the end of most of my workshops for nonprofit leaders, I ask the attendees to take out their calendars, look at the following week, and block off time for themselves—what I call "selfish space." There is always hesitation.

Especially for nonprofit leaders whose personal missions are so closely tied to their professional ones, the idea of putting their own needs ahead of others sometimes feels uncomfortable. I remember one leader specifically saying, "I could never do that without feeling guilty." So, I reiterated the research. Taking care of yourself is not about ignoring responsibilities; it is about creating space to recharge so you can serve better, both at work and at home.

One leader, in particular, called me weeks after a workshop and said she is now on her eleventh scheduled selfish-space activity and seeing the impact. She was "more focused" and "less stressed," and her team began "noticing the change" too. She added new activities—like playing with her dog and painting—intermittently in her day. Each activity brought a different kind of recharge, allowing her to reconnect with her mission more effectively.

Contrast this example with another leader's story who cut a family vacation short because of an issue at work. She was praised for her commitment, even receiving a recognition plaque as a joke. But her team felt disempowered because she returned early, her family felt abandoned because she prioritized work over vacation, and the organization's board privately wondered how long she could keep up this pace.

My research on "selfish space" shows that variety and frequency are key for maximum effectiveness—finding a good mix of activities that replenish you and sprinkling these moments throughout your day, week, month, and year. It could be as simple as taking a walk in nature, going for a run, reading a book, grabbing lunch with a friend, or sitting quietly with your thoughts.

Selfish space isn't selfish at all. It's the cornerstone of being ready and willing to serve others effectively.

Creating Your Own Space for Self-Care

Finding selfish space is essential for maintaining your mental and emotional wellbeing in a world that constantly demands your attention. It's not about being selfish in a negative way but about creating a sanctuary for yourself where you can recharge and reflect. Let's see how well you're doing in this area.

Ask yourself the following questions and rate yourself from 0 to 5, with 0 being "Never," 1 "Rarely," 2 "Sometimes," 3 "Often," 4 "Usually," and 5 "Always":

_____ I am happy with the air quality, light, and noise at my home.

_____ I have a calm, uncluttered space I can often go to for relaxation.

_____ I have an activity or practice that allows me to periodically 'clear' my head.

_____ I am comfortable spending time alone with my thoughts.

_____ I think positively of myself.

_____ **TOTAL**

Now, take all your numbers and add them up to get your total score. For example, if you rated yourself a four in every area, your total score would be 20. Here's how to interpret your results:

- 21 - 25: Outstanding! You have a strong sense of maintaining selfish space. Keep nurturing this sanctuary to sustain your wellbeing.

- 16 - 20: You're on the right track, but there's room for improvement. Focus on the areas where you scored lower to enhance your personal space.

- 15 or below: Don't worry. It's never too late to start creating a space for yourself.

Remember, creating selfish space isn't about neglecting others; it's about ensuring you have the energy and clarity to be your best self. Here are some actions to help you find and nurture your sanctuary:

Mindfulness Meditation: Dedicate 5 to 10 minutes each day to practice a mindfulness meditation. Find a quiet spot, focus on your breath, and ignore distracting thoughts. This practice can help clear your mind and reduce stress. There are plenty of mobile apps and online videos to help you accomplish this one.

Create a Calm Space: Identify a small area in your home as your relaxation zone. Keep it uncluttered and fill it with things that make you feel calm, like candles, soft lighting, a cozy chair, soothing music, plants, essential oils, soft blankets, calming artwork, and your favorite books. Retreat to this space when needed. Maybe even practice your mindfulness meditation there.

Schedule "Me Time": Look at the following week in your calendar and block time for yourself. Use this time to do something you enjoy, whether it's reading, taking a walk, napping, or simply sitting quietly. Treat this time as non-negotiable. Leave time at the end of the activity to schedule the next one for a week out.

Engage in these activities, and you'll feel more centered, focused, and ready to take on the world by prioritizing your space and time.

Go FurtherFaster in Your Environmental Wellbeing

Environmental Wellbeing is about creating and maintaining a safe, sustainable, and supportive environment that nurtures your growth and health. This section explored two critical principles for enhancing your Environmental Wellbeing: Give Things Away and Find Selfish Space.

Give Things Away: This principle emphasizes the power of generosity and community engagement. By sharing your time, skills, and resources with others, you enrich the lives of those around you and your own. Acts of giving strengthen a sense of connection and purpose, reminding us that our actions have a broader impact. Generosity is not just about material gifts; it's about creating a supportive environment where everyone can thrive.

Find Selfish Space: This principle focuses on the importance of carving out time and space for yourself to recharge and rejuvenate. In a world that constantly demands your attention, having a personal sanctuary—whether a physical space or a mental practice—is essential for managing stress. Prioritizing your own needs is not selfish; it's necessary for sustaining the energy required to care for others and contribute meaningfully to your environment.

These principles are complementary, each enhancing the other. By integrating these principles, you create a sustainable approach to living that supports your journey toward a thriving and accomplished life.

Section 3
Financial Wellbeing

Financial Wellbeing reflects the quality of your relationship with money, encompassing both the freedom to make choices and the security that comes from financial stability. It's about managing your current income and expenses while also preparing for the future by growing wealth and building financial resilience.

Whether you have a modest income or substantial wealth, understanding and managing your finances is essential for achieving stability and peace of mind. Financial Wellbeing requires prioritizing two key principles: developing long-term saving strategies and creating short-term spending plans that allow you to enjoy life today. These are the foundations of the FurtherFaster approach to Financial Wellbeing.

To Go Further: Save Some Money

Saving money is essential for securing your financial future and protecting yourself from unexpected expenses. Without a solid savings plan, you face the risk of financial instability and stress during emergencies or retirement. Prioritizing saving—paying yourself first—ensures that you are consistently building wealth for the future. It's a core driver of financial freedom and long-term success.

To Go Faster: Spend Some Money

Spending money thoughtfully on meaningful experiences and essential needs today allows you to enjoy the fruits of your hard work. Purposeful spending enhances your quality of life, bringing joy and fulfillment. Neglecting to spend on the present can leave you feeling deprived and disconnected, missing out on experiences that bring immediate value and satisfaction.

Achieving the right mix between these two principles—saving for tomorrow and spending for today—is key to financial health and happiness. Saving money lays the foundation for a secure future, while spending wisely enriches your life in the present. Let's explore these principles to enhance your Financial Wellbeing.

Further Principle

Save Some Money

"Money isn't the most important thing in life, but it's reasonably close to oxygen on the 'gotta have it' scale."

- Zig Ziglar

Saving some money involves deliberately setting aside a portion of your income for future use. It's not just about stashing cash away—it's about cultivating a mindset of financial prudence, foresight, and discipline. Those who consistently save demonstrate self-regulation and patience, prioritizing long-term benefits over short-term pleasures. These individuals—often labeled "savers"—understand that financial stability isn't about how much you earn but how much you keep and manage wisely.

Research underscores the significance of this principle. For instance, a 2023 Forbes Advisor survey found that 43% of Americans have never opened a high-yield savings account, despite the potential for these accounts to significantly enhance savings through higher interest rates [15]. This missed opportunity for financial growth suggests a possible gap in financial literacy or a lack of understanding about the benefits of saving. While there are other factors, such as education, which creates access to higher pay, or inflation, which impacts buying power, many who don't save may have never had strong financial role models to instill these habits early on. No matter the circumstance, if we're not engaged in diligent saving practices, we're missing out on the compounding effects.

In addition, the personal savings rate in the US has been declining, hovering around 4.6% in the last few years, which is below a decades-long average of roughly 8.9% [16]. This decline indicates that many Americans struggle to set aside money, often living paycheck to paycheck due to difficult circumstances or making poor choices of prioritizing immediate expenses over future security.

These statistics highlight a critical issue facing many Americans today: the lack of sufficient savings for future security. However, it's important to consider that by building a habit of regular saving, you protect yourself against unforeseen expenses and position yourself for long-term stability and peace of mind.

The Value of Thinking Long-Term

I've always believed in the importance of saving money for the future, but it wasn't until I started working closely with my personal investment advisor that this belief turned into consistent action. Over the last decade, there have been countless times when I was tempted to dip into our long-term investments to cover immediate needs or desires. *What's the harm*, I thought? After all, I had saved that money for the future, and sometimes it felt like the future was now.

There were many tempting moments: a costly truck engine repair, new furniture for the house, an unexpectedly large tax bill, and even a much-needed family vacation. Each time, I considered withdrawing a significant amount from my retirement funds to cover these expenses. However, each time I approached my advisor with this idea, he skillfully talked me down. He ran the numbers and showed me that taking on some short-term debt would be less harmful than jeopardizing my financial future, outlining the long-term impact of pulling from my savings, fees, and tax consequences.

My investment advisor's guidance was a perfect embodiment of the principle. By encouraging me to think long-term and avoid quick fixes through premature withdrawals, he reinforced the value of prioritizing long-term stability over short-term comfort.

These experiences have taught me that saving money is about more than just creating a cushion for emergencies or ensuring a comfortable retirement. It's about building a solid foundation for future opportunities and stability. Thanks to this lesson and the continued diligence in following it, I now see saving as an act of future-proofing our lives—a critical strategy for ensuring both security and the freedom to pursue opportunities when they arise.

Saving money requires discipline and the foresight to recognize that short-term sacrifices lead to long-term gains.

Building Your Financial Safety Net

Whether you're preparing for emergencies, planning for a significant purchase, or looking ahead to retirement, having a strong savings strategy is key. Let's assess how well you're doing with your savings habits.

Ask yourself the following questions and rate yourself from 0 to 5, with 0 being "Never," 1 "Rarely," 2 "Sometimes," 3 "Often," 4 "Usually," and 5 "Always":

_____ I have a steady income or regularly accumulate money and resources.

_____ I consistently set aside a portion of my income for future needs.

_____ I have money set aside that I can access immediately in case of an emergency.

_____ I plan and forecast financially either by myself or with an advisor for the long term.

_____ I have a growing reserve or nest egg of money or resources set aside.

_____ **TOTAL**

Now, take all your numbers and add them up to get your total score. For example, if you rated yourself a four in every area, your total score would be 20. Here's how to interpret your results:

- 21 - 25: Excellent! You have a strong foundation in saving money. Continue to build on this strength to enhance your financial security.

- 16 - 20: Good job, but there's room for improvement. Focus on areas where you scored lower to strengthen your savings habits.

- 15 or below: Don't worry. Now is a great time to start making changes to improve your savings strategy.

No matter where you score, saving money is a skill that can be developed and refined over time. Here are some actions you can take to improve your savings habits:

Track Your Spending: Use a budgeting app to monitor your daily expenses for one month. Identify areas where you can cut back and allocate those funds to savings. Understanding where your money goes is the first step toward better financial management.

Automate Your Savings: Set up an automatic monthly transfer from your checking account to your savings account. Start with a small amount that you can easily manage and gradually increase it over time. Automation ensures that saving becomes a consistent habit.

Build an Emergency Fund: Start by saving at least $1,000 for emergencies. Once you reach this initial goal, aim to save three to six months' worth of living expenses. An emergency fund acts as a financial buffer, giving you peace of mind for unexpected expenses [17].

Remember, by integrating these practices into your life, you'll build a stronger financial foundation and be better prepared for whatever life throws at you. Every little bit saved adds up over time, leading to greater financial security and freedom.

Faster Principle

Spend Some Money

"A budget is telling your money where to go instead of wondering where it went."

- Dave Ramsey

Spending some money isn't about indulgence or thoughtless purchases; it's about making deliberate, mindful choices with your finances to enhance your life and wellbeing. This principle is about investing in experiences and items that bring joy, improve quality of life, and support personal and professional growth. Rather than frivolous spending, it's about making expenditures that are aligned with your values and bring genuine fulfillment [18].

A person who embodies this principle understands the struggle between financial responsibility and the enjoyment of their earnings. They are mindful of budgeting for necessities while also setting aside funds for activities and purchases that bring happiness and enrichment. This could include investing in travel, engaging in hobbies, pursuing further education, or occasionally treating themselves to something special. By making thoughtful spending choices, they maximize both their present enjoyment and long-term satisfaction.

Research supports this approach. A study by Cornell University found that people who spent money on experiences rather than material goods reported significantly higher levels of happiness and life satisfaction. The study highlighted that experiential purchases, like vacations or concerts, provide more enduring pleasure compared to material items, which tend to lose their appeal quickly after the initial purchase [19].

Moreover, a 2021 survey by Gallup revealed that Americans who spend on discretionary purchases—such as dining out, entertainment, and travel—tend to report higher overall wellbeing than those who limit their spending to basic needs [20]. This suggests that spending on experiences and enjoyable activities is closely linked to improved mental health and life satisfaction.

Spending money wisely—on experiences and activities that enrich life—can lead to greater satisfaction and wellbeing. It's not just about how much you spend but where and how you choose to invest your financial resources. By prioritizing meaningful expenditures, you can enjoy the present while building a fulfilling, well-rounded life.

Planning for Tomorrow with Joy for Today

While saving for the future is undeniably important, there's also immense value in enjoying the present. Growing up, my family had a tradition: We would celebrate with a treat whenever there was a financial windfall—a raise, a bonus, or a tax refund. Sometimes, it was as simple as a candy bar. Other times, it was something more extravagant, like a family vacation. This tradition taught me a valuable lesson about finding joy in the here and now.

I vividly remember one particular year when my parents received a substantial tax refund. Instead of squirreling it all away into savings, they chose to take us on a memorable family trip. During that trip, we didn't hear "We can't do that" or "You can't have that." We experienced new things, spent quality time together, and created lasting memories. This wasn't about being frivolous; it was about living life to its fullest and understanding that money, while a tool for future security, can also be a means to enjoy the present.

Not everyone can take grand vacations or spend freely; we must be mindful of our financial limits. But the core idea remains: Life isn't just about preparing for tomorrow—it's also about making today count.

It's about finding that sweet spot where financial prudence meets life's pleasures. So, don't hesitate to spend some money on what truly matters to you and those you love. After all, the memories you create today are an investment in happiness that can last a lifetime.

Spending Wisely for a Fulfilling Life

While saving money is essential for financial security, spending money thoughtfully and enjoying the rewards of your hard work is just as important. Let's assess your spending habits to see how well you're managing your finances while enjoying life.

Ask yourself the following questions and rate yourself from 0 to 5, with 0 being "Never," 1 "Rarely," 2 "Sometimes," 3 "Often," 4 "Usually," and 5 "Always":

_____ I have a detailed spending plan and strategy for managing my finances.

_____ I feel comfortable with my current amount of debt.

_____ I do not deprive myself of basic needs due to financial concerns.

_____ I make informed financial decisions that align with my current needs and future goals.

_____ I am resourceful and creative with my money and resources.

_____ **TOTAL**

Now, take all your numbers and add them up to get your total score. For example, if you rated yourself a four in every area, your total score would be 20. Here's how to interpret your results:

- 21 - 25: Fantastic! You have a healthy mix between saving and spending. Keep nurturing these habits to maintain Financial Wellbeing and enjoy life to the fullest.

- 16 - 20: Good job, but there's room for improvement. Consider focusing on areas where you scored lower to better manage your spending while enjoying life.

- 15 or below: Don't worry. There are always ways to adjust your spending habits for a healthier financial life.

Remember, spending money doesn't mean being reckless; it's about being intentional and making choices that enhance your life. Here are some actions to help you manage your spending while enjoying your earnings:

Create a Realistic Budget: Develop a budget that suits your lifestyle. Include categories for essentials, savings, and discretionary spending. This will help you track your spending and ensure you're not overspending in any area [21].

Plan for Enjoyment: Allocate a portion of your budget for fun and leisure activities. Whether it's dining out, traveling, or buying something special, enjoying your money responsibly can enhance your overall wellbeing.

Practice Mindful Spending: Before making a purchase, consider if it aligns with your values and long-term goals.

Ask yourself if it will bring lasting joy or is a temporary impulse. Regularly check your budget and spending habits. Make adjustments as needed to stay on track with your financial goals while allowing yourself to enjoy life.

By finding the right mix between saving and spending, you can achieve financial stability while living a fulfilling life. Remember, it's about making the most of your money in a way that enhances your overall happiness and wellbeing.

Go FurtherFaster in Your Financial Wellbeing

Financial Wellbeing is a cornerstone of a secure and fulfilling life. It's not just about accumulating wealth but about managing your money in a way that supports both your present needs and future aspirations. This section explored two essential principles for achieving Financial Wellbeing: Save Some Money and Spend Some Money.

Save Some Money: This principle emphasizes the importance of financial discipline and planning for the future. By setting aside money for emergencies, major purchases, or retirement, you build a safety net that provides peace of mind and financial security. Cultivating the habit of saving ensures that you are prepared to face unexpected challenges and pursue long-term goals with confidence.

Spend Some Money: This principle focuses on the value of enjoying your resources in the present. It encourages mindful spending on experiences and purchases that bring joy and enrich your life. Spending money in this manner is about being intentional with your money—using it to create meaningful moments and enhance your quality of life while still maintaining financial responsibility.

Together, these two principles offer a comprehensive approach to Financial Wellbeing. Saving money provides the foundation for long-term security, while spending wisely allows you to savor life in the present.

By integrating both principles into your financial strategy, you can navigate the complexities of money management with greater clarity, stability, and fulfillment.

Section 4
Intellectual Wellbeing

Intellectual Wellbeing goes beyond simply acquiring knowledge; it's about staying curious, engaging in complex thoughts, and remaining open to new ideas that challenge your perspectives. It nurtures mental agility, sharpens critical thinking, and fuels lifelong curiosity, keeping your mind sharp and adaptable in an ever-changing world. Intellectual Wellbeing equips you to solve problems effectively, innovate, and stay resilient.

We need to embrace both foundational knowledge and forward-thinking innovation to strengthen our Intellectual Wellbeing.

To illustrate these ideas, let's learn more about these FurtherFaster Principles and explore how they contribute to thriving Intellectual Wellbeing.

To Go Further: Understand Basic Things

Building a solid foundation of basic knowledge is key to long-term cognitive health and effective problem-solving [22]. Without this fundamental understanding, complex tasks can become overwhelming, and learning new concepts becomes more challenging. If you don't grasp the basics of what's happening around you right now, you may struggle to progress, and others may hesitate to bring you along on their journey.

To Go Faster: Disrupt Traditional Methods

Disrupting traditional methods fosters rapid innovation and mental stimulation. By challenging conventional approaches and embracing new ideas, you unlock new possibilities and break free from outdated ways of thinking. If you neglect to innovate, you risk becoming stagnant and stuck in the same routines as everyone else.

Both of these principles are key to long-term intellectual success, and it's critical to recognize that these principles only work when used together. If you focus solely on mastering the basics without seeking innovation, you may find yourself stuck in outdated methods, unable to adapt to change. On the other hand, if you focus solely on innovation without a strong foundation, you risk moving forward without a clear direction.

Let's unpack each of these principles to enhance your Intellectual Wellbeing.

Further Principle

Understand Basic Things

"Common sense is not so common."

- Voltaire

Understanding basic things involves mastering fundamental concepts and practical knowledge that guide everyday decisions and actions. This principle emphasizes the importance of common sense and critical thinking in navigating life's complexities effectively. It is about being grounded in reality, making informed choices, and solving problems efficiently.

A person who embodies this principle is both observant and analytical. They strive to understand how things work, why certain events occur, and what actions can improve a given situation. This foundational knowledge enables them to solve problems quickly and easily adapt to changing circumstances. Their ability to draw on "common sense" allows them to come up with solutions to unexpected challenges in their daily lives and support those around them.

Also, their practical wisdom provides them with the confidence to make sound decisions and act decisively in a variety of scenarios.

Research supports the significance of this principle. It's been proven that children and adults feel more self-sufficient and independent when they can fix or maintain things around their homes without relying on assistance from others [23]. This implies that understanding basic things can enhance one's sense of capability and power over one's life.

Further reinforcing this idea, a study by La Trobe University found that individuals who can perform basic household tasks experience significant improvements in executive functions in the workplace. [24]. This suggests that practical skills and problem-solving abilities are highly valued in professional settings.

Also, research shows that individuals with higher "practical intelligence"—the ability to understand and navigate everyday situations—earn an average of $29,000 more per year than those who lack these fundamental life skills [25]. These findings highlight the tangible financial and professional benefits of mastering simple, practical skills.

Whether it's feeling independent, achieving workplace gains, or having more money, understanding basic things clearly has personal and professional value.

The Confidence of Common Sense

While studying computer science in college, I worked as a licensed home inspector to help support myself. I spent countless hours navigating attics and crawl spaces, testing outlets and hot water tanks, and learning more about furnaces and electrical boxes than most people ever will. These practical experiences were more than just a job; they were lessons in understanding how things work and how to solve everyday problems.

When I came home or when friends, family, and neighbors needed handyman help, I was often the go-to person. I could wire, fit, route, and repair just about anything, saving myself and those I helped literally thousands of dollars. This knowledge of how a house functions and the ability to identify just about everything in a hardware store has served me well throughout my life.

This is knowledge I certainly wanted to pass on to my kids. But one day, after living for years in a newly constructed home, I realized my oldest son didn't know the difference between a flathead and a Phillips screwdriver. That's when my wife and I decided it was time for a change. We moved from our modern home to a 1929 fixer-upper, where the basics of home repair would become a family affair. Weekends are now spent sealing windows, repairing appliances, and tackling basic plumbing and electrical tasks. Now, my sons are familiar with our tool shed and have a growing confidence in their abilities to fix things.

They are learning the importance of understanding how things work and gaining the skills to handle everyday challenges. They are building a foundation of practical knowledge that will serve them well beyond our weekend projects.

Understanding basic things, whatever you consider to be important, is about building confidence, growing a sense of independence, and equipping yourself with the skills to navigate life's everyday hurdles. It's a lesson I hope everyone embraces, learning more each day about the value of mastering the basics.

Level Up Your Everyday Skills

Understanding basic things is about mastering practical knowledge and applying common sense to navigate everyday situations effectively. Let's assess how well you grasp the essentials and where you might need to improve.

Ask yourself the following questions and rate yourself from 0 to 5, with 0 being "Never," 1 "Rarely," 2 "Sometimes," 3 "Often," 4 "Usually," and 5 "Always":

- ____ I stay informed about national, societal, and global issues.

- ____ I actively work to improve my writing and verbal communication skills.

- ____ I engage in conversations with people who offer practical insights.

_____ I regularly put myself in situations that require everyday problem-solving.

_____ I reflect on my decisions to understand what went well and what could be improved.

_____ **TOTAL**

Now, take all your numbers and add them up to get your total score. For example, if you rated yourself a four in every area, your total score would be 20. Here's how to interpret your results:

- 21 - 25: Excellent! You have a strong grasp of the basics and are well-equipped to handle everyday challenges. Keep building on this solid foundation.

- 16 - 20: You're doing well, but there's room for growth. Consider focusing on the areas where you scored lower to enhance your understanding and application of basic knowledge.

- 15 or below: Don't worry. There are always opportunities to improve your practical skills and knowledge.

Having a solid grasp of practical knowledge can boost your confidence and efficiency in daily life. Here are three steps to help you enhance your understanding of basic things:

Commit to Lifelong Learning: Dedicate time each week to learning something new. This could be reading articles, watching educational videos, or enrolling in a course on a topic that interests you. Continuous learning keeps your mind sharp and well-informed.

Engage in Practical Projects: Take on small projects that require practical skills. This could be fixing something around the house, cooking a new recipe, or building something from scratch. These activities enhance your problem-solving abilities and build confidence in handling everyday tasks.

Reflect and Apply Your Knowledge: At the end of each day, take a few moments to reflect on what you've learned and how you've applied it. Consider the decisions you made, what went well, and where you could improve. This daily reflection reinforces your learning and helps you apply basic knowledge more effectively.

By committing to understanding and mastering the basics, you'll become more capable and confident in handling everyday challenges, leading to a more efficient and fulfilling life.

Faster Principle

Disrupt Traditional Methods

"If you always do what you've always done, you'll always get what you've always got."

- Henry Ford

Disrupting traditional methods involves challenging the status quo and exploring innovative approaches to achieve better results. This principle is about questioning established practices and seeking new, more effective ways to accomplish tasks and solve problems. It's about breaking free from the constraints of "how things have always been done" and finding new paths forward.

A person who embodies this principle is naturally curious and open-minded. They are not satisfied with simply following the established ways; instead, they actively seek opportunities to improve and innovate. This mindset often involves experimenting with new ideas, learning from failures, and continuously adapting strategies to find what works best. Such individuals are frequently seen as trailblazers and change-makers, inspiring others to think differently and embrace new possibilities.

The impact of disrupting traditional methods is not just theoretical but backed by substantial research. For example, a study published by the *Harvard Business Review* found that companies that embraced unconventional approaches and moved beyond traditional methods were significantly more likely to achieve breakthrough innovation than their more conventional competitors [26]. This demonstrates that challenging the status quo and encouraging a culture of innovation is necessary for organizations aiming to achieve remarkable progress.

Moreover, a McKinsey survey conducted during the COVID-19 pandemic highlighted that organizations that were quickest to adapt and implement non-traditional methods of strategizing, communicating, and working saw higher revenue growth compared to those that stuck with conventional approaches. This finding underscores the critical role that flexibility and innovative thinking play in navigating crises and achieving rapid growth.

Further evidence from McKinsey shows that companies led by CEOs who actively encouraged employees to question traditional practices and explore unconventional solutions were:

- 10x Faster at Developing New Products: Top innovators are faster than their less innovative counterparts in launching new products.

- 6x More Effective at Scaling New Businesses: These companies lead the charge in scaling new businesses, enabling them to grow faster.

- 3x More Likely to Meet Customer Needs: Innovative organizations are more likely to align their offerings with customer demands [28].

These insights make it clear: Disrupting the boundaries of traditional practices is not just about personal or organizational growth—it's about driving significant, lasting change. These findings collectively highlight the significant impact that challenging established norms and creating a culture of innovation can have on achieving success and driving positive change.

The Innovator's Instinct

I've always had a knack for questioning the status quo. It's not just about finding flaws but about seeking better ways to achieve results.

One day, while riding in the car with my wife, we stopped at a red light. I noticed someone washing their car nearby, starting from the bottom of the driver's side door and working their way up. I couldn't help but blurt out, "What is he doing? Start at the top. The water runs down, breaks up the mud, and keeps the bucket water from getting as dirty."

I turned to my wife, expecting her agreement, but instead, she just looked at me and said with a half-amused, half-exasperated expression, "You can't shut it off, can you?"

No, I can't.

This constant questioning of methods and seeking improvements has been a driving force in my life. It's not just about challenging others but challenging myself and the systems around me. This mindset has led to many innovative ideas, companies, and opportunities. In fact, the *Texas Medical Center* magazine once named me one of the top 12 innovators in the Houston TMC for my work at the hospital systems there. This recognition wasn't just for sticking with the norm; it was because of my relentless pursuit of more effective and innovative approaches to problems.

Disrupting traditional methods is about challenging the norm and thinking outside the box. This approach has opened doors and created opportunities I never imagined possible, and it can do the same for you.

Think Beyond the Box

Innovation thrives when we challenge the status quo and disrupt traditional methods. Let's see how open you are to embracing an innovative mindset.

Ask yourself the following questions and rate yourself from 0 to 5, with 0 being "Never," 1 "Rarely," 2 "Sometimes," 3 "Often," 4 "Usually," and 5 "Always":

_____ I actively seek out opportunities to learn new things.

_____ I gather information from various sources before making decisions.

_____ I regularly ask others for their perspectives to broaden my understanding.

_____ I keep sources of inspiration, like books or podcasts, around me.

_____ I think of multiple ways to solve an issue before taking action.

_____ **TOTAL**

Now, take all your numbers and add them up to get your total score. For example, if you rated yourself a four in every area, your total score would be 20. Here's how to interpret your results:

- 21 - 25: Fantastic! You have a strong inclination toward innovation and are constantly looking for ways to improve. Keep nurturing this innovative mindset.

- 16 - 20: You're on the right path, but there's room for more creativity. Focus on areas where you scored lower to cultivate your innovative approach further.

- 15 or below: It's never too late to start thinking outside the box. Start small and gradually build your innovation skills.

Remember, innovation isn't only about groundbreaking discoveries; it's about making everyday improvements that can lead to significant results. Here are some steps to help you disrupt traditional methods and spark innovation:

Innovation Switch Challenge: Take a routine task you perform regularly and brainstorm an entirely new way to complete it. This could involve using a different tool, changing the order of steps, or adding a creative twist. Implement this new method and observe its impact on your efficiency and enjoyment.

Diverse Perspectives: Expose yourself to a variety of viewpoints by reading books, watching documentaries, or following thought leaders from different fields. This diversity can inspire new ideas and help you see problems from a different angle.

Collaborative Brainstorming: Engage in brainstorming sessions with friends, family, or colleagues. Encourage everyone to share their wildest, most unconventional ideas without judgment. This collaborative environment can lead to innovative solutions and fresh perspectives.

By incorporating these practices into your life, you'll cultivate a mindset of continuous improvement and innovation, helping you disrupt traditional ways of thinking for greater personal and professional fulfillment.

Go FurtherFaster in Your Intellectual Wellbeing

Intellectual Wellbeing goes beyond merely acquiring knowledge; it's about cultivating curiosity, critical thinking, and a mindset of continuous growth. By engaging your mind in meaningful ways, you enhance your cognitive abilities and enrich your life with fresh perspectives and insights. In this section, we explored two essential principles to elevate your Intellectual Wellbeing: Understand Basic Things and Disrupt Traditional Methods.

Understand Basic Things: This principle is about mastering the foundational knowledge and practical skills that are essential for navigating everyday life. Embracing basic tasks encourages you to stay informed, hone your problem-solving skills, and actively engage with the world. Whether it's managing finances, understanding current events, or performing simple tasks, a strong grasp of the basics builds your confidence and empowers you to tackle life's challenges with ease.

Disrupting Traditional Methods: This principle challenges you to go beyond conventional wisdom and embrace innovation. By questioning existing practices and exploring new approaches, you cultivate creativity and unlock new possibilities for personal and professional growth. Being innovative drives you to think outside the box, challenge the status quo, and continuously seek out more effective solutions to achieve your goals.

Together, these two principles form a powerful framework for intellectual growth. Understanding basic things provides a solid foundation of knowledge and skills, while disrupting traditional methods empowers you to innovate and build on that foundation with creative problem-solving. This dynamic combination helps you stay adaptable, informed, and ahead of the curve so you can go FurtherFaster.

Section 5
Organizational Wellbeing

Organizational Wellbeing refers to a person's ability to structure various aspects of their life to minimize stress and maximize efficiency. This type of wellbeing is characterized by decluttering physical and mental spaces, maintaining a sharp focus, meeting commitments reliably, and swiftly adapting to unexpected changes.

Organizational Wellbeing is more than just keeping your environment tidy or sticking to a routine—it's about cultivating systems and habits that support ongoing efficiency, productivity, and a sense of calm. When your life is organized, it enables you to perform at your best, even in the face of life's inevitable challenges. Organizational Wellbeing is a core element in ensuring you can manage multiple responsibilities while staying focused and resilient, allowing for smoother transitions between personal, professional, and social demands.

To achieve this, Organizational Wellbeing hinges on two key principles: Remaining Highly Adaptable and Wasting No Time. Adaptability allows you to remain resilient and composed when facing unexpected changes, while efficient time management ensures that every moment is used effectively, minimizing stress and maximizing output. These principles work together to give you mastery over your environment and your approach to life's challenges. Let's take a closer look at them.

To Go Further: Remain Highly Adaptable

Adaptability is the ability to adjust to new conditions while maintaining your core values and objectives. This capacity is essential for ensuring long-term success, as it allows you to handle unexpected challenges and pivot your strategies when necessary. In a constantly evolving world, being adaptable helps you stay relevant, resilient, and prepared for whatever comes your way. Without adaptability, you may find it difficult to cope with surprises, leading to increased stress and decreased efficiency. Being too rigid can cause you to miss opportunities and struggle to recover from setbacks. By remaining highly adaptable, you navigate challenges without losing your footing, ensuring that you are always prepared for the unexpected and able to continue moving forward, even when conditions are less than ideal.

To Go Faster: Waste No Time

Efficient time management is key to achieving immediate productivity and reaching your goals. Wherever you are on your time management journey—whether you're just beginning to tackle distractions, somewhere in the middle, or already a seasoned planner—there's always room to improve and refine your approach. By focusing on high-priority tasks and cutting out activities that drain your time, you can steadily become more productive and feel more in control. It's not about perfection but about progress. Taking small, consistent steps will help you move from scrambling to meet deadlines to staying ahead of them. As you refine your skills, the benefits are immediate: reduced stress, more opportunities seized, and the ability to tackle each day with confidence. The process begins wherever you are now, and with practice, you'll waste less time and accomplish more without the constant feeling of playing catch-up.

In essence, Organizational Wellbeing is about adaptability with structure. Adaptability promotes long-term success by enabling you to adjust to changes, while a well-structured approach ensures that you make the most of your time and maintain immediate productivity. Organizational Wellbeing acts as the foundation that helps you maintain clarity and resilience over the multiple facets of your life, supporting you in sustaining momentum, reducing stress, and handling life's complexities with greater ease.

Further Principle

Remain Highly Adaptable

"The snake which cannot cast its skin has to die. As well the minds which are prevented from changing their opinions; they cease to be."

- Friedrich Nietzsche

Remaining highly adaptable involves being open to change, allowing you to adjust your plans and actions as circumstances evolve. However, adaptability is not just about reacting to change; it's about proactively embracing it as a pathway to growth and resilience. This principle emphasizes agility in both thought and behavior, enabling you to navigate uncertainty with confidence and ease.

A person who embodies this principle views change not as a threat but as an opportunity to learn and grow. Embracing new situations with a positive attitude, they can quickly pivot in response to unexpected challenges or new opportunities. And their ability to remain calm and effective amid uncertainty makes them valuable assets in any environment—personal or professional.

In fact, according to a study by the University of Phoenix, over 75% of employers prioritize creativity, forward-thinking, innovation, and adaptability over technical skills when hiring new employees. This shift reflects the growing recognition that in a rapidly changing world, the ability to adapt to new situations is more critical than ever [29].

And not just at work. Adaptability is equally influential in our personal lives. A study performed by researchers at the University of Surrey showed that even the perception of how adaptable we are, or are allowed to be, significantly impacts how we feel about ourselves [30].

It's like Charles Darwin alluded to in his book, *Origin of Species*, about success and survival. It's not necessarily the strongest or the smartest who thrive but those who can adapt to change. So, adaptability isn't just an advantage; it's a necessity.

By cultivating a mindset that welcomes change, we position ourselves to seize new opportunities, overcome obstacles, and, ultimately, thrive in any environment.

Luck Through Adaptability

Luck is often seen as random chance—a serendipitous event that falls into your lap. People sometimes ask me if I believe in luck. Surprisingly, I do, but not in the way most people think.

For me, luck is not mere chance; it's a combination of positioning and preparation.

Positioning: Being in the right place at the right time is often seen as luck, but it's really about positioning yourself where opportunities are likely to arise. This means putting yourself in the right situations—attending events, making connections, and staying open to new experiences.

Preparation: When an opportunity comes out of the blue, it can easily pass you by if you're not ready to seize it. Preparing yourself for potential opportunities—those "lucky breaks"—makes all the difference.

For example, my wife and I made a pivotal decision early in our lives to move away from our families and embrace an out-of-state opportunity. This decision set off a chain reaction of other opportunities—each one requiring us to remain adaptable and open to change. Because we maintained a highly adaptable mindset, we ended up living in and visiting various states and countries, each experience adding richness to our lives and careers.

Of course, this principle isn't limited to geographic moves or career changes; it applies equally to relationships, financial decisions, and more. By remaining highly adaptable, you'll find that "luck" is often the result of your readiness to embrace whatever comes your way.

Adaptability for a Dynamic Life

In a constantly changing world, adaptability is key to staying resilient and making the most of new opportunities. Let's assess how adaptable you are in managing life's surprises and shifts.

Ask yourself the following questions and rate yourself from 0 to 5, with 0 being "Never," 1 "Rarely," 2 "Sometimes," 3 "Often," 4 "Usually," and 5 "Always":

____ I can quickly adapt my plans or priorities based on changing circumstances.

____ I leave some contingency time in my schedule to handle unexpected events.

____ I am not often upset when plans change or someone cancels on me.

____ I regularly seek new approaches and different methods to stay adaptable.

____ I can see an opportunity in most challenges or problems I face.

____ **TOTAL**

Now, take all your numbers and add them up to get your total score. For example, if you rated yourself a four in every area, your total score would be 20. Here's how to interpret your results:

- 21 - 25: Excellent! You are highly adaptable to life's changes. Keep nurturing this trait to maintain your resilience.

- 16 - 20: You're doing well, but there's room for improvement. Focus on the areas where you scored lower to enhance your adaptability.

- 15 or below: It's a great time to start embracing adaptability. Begin with small changes to build a more adaptable mindset.

Being adaptable doesn't mean being unstructured; it means being prepared and equipped to handle the unexpected. Having a system in place actually makes it easier to adapt because it frees up mental energy and time for flexibility. When you're more organized, you can respond to changes and seize new opportunities with less stress, knowing your core responsibilities are under control.

Here are three steps to help you build adaptability into your daily life while keeping your foundational structure intact:

Change Your Routine: Introduce a small change to your daily routine, like taking a new route to work, rearranging your workspace, or engaging in a different type of exercise. Notice how this simple shift influences your day and your perspective.

Set an Unusual Goal: Challenge yourself with a goal outside your usual comfort zone, such as learning a new language, participating in a community event, or starting a creative project. Focus on the journey and adaptation rather than just the outcome.

Embrace New Opportunities: Say "yes" to an opportunity you would normally pass up. This could be anything from a new project at work to a social event or a hobby. Embracing these moments can help develop a more adaptable and open mindset.

By incorporating these practices, you'll enhance your adaptability and resilience, better preparing you for whatever life throws your way.

Faster Principle

Waste No Time

"The way to get started is to quit talking and begin doing."

- Walt Disney

Wasting no time is about maximizing every moment to focus on meaningful and productive activities. It involves prioritizing tasks that align with your goals and values while eliminating distractions and unnecessary activities. And it's a skill that anyone can learn over time with practice and intentional effort.

However, several striking facts illustrate how much time is actually being wasted by those with poor time management skills. According to the *New York Post* and the McKinsey Global Institute (respectively):

- The average person spends about 2.5 days per year searching for misplaced items [31].

- The average employee spends an average of 1.8 hours per day—over 9 hours per week—searching for information needed to perform their jobs effectively [32].

And this is just one aspect of time management—placing items and files where you can easily find them! Imagine what would happen if we collectively got better at managing our time. If we just improved or cut out inefficient meetings, we'd not only save the US economy an estimated $399 billion annually in lost productivity, but we'd also be able to create more fulfilling and productive companies and ultimately lead happier, healthier lives [33].

Every Second Counts

I despise wasting time. Whether I'm working at my desk, at home, in a classroom, in a shared office space, or in a small and busy area, as soon as I enter it, I make sure everything I need is organized and easy to find. A place for everything and everything in its place. This mindset carries through all areas of my life, not just my workspace.

To help manage my time effectively, I've developed a system that keeps me focused no matter where I am. On my dedicated work desk, I use an eight-sided Bluetooth-connected die, with each side representing a different aspect of my day—like working on a client project, creating slides for teaching, working on a business idea, or even writing. When I flip the die, it logs my time for that specific activity automatically until I turn it to another side. If I'm not at my desk, I use an app to track my tasks on the go. This system helps me allocate where my time is spent, and I set alarms to remind me when I'm spending too much time on one thing or not enough on another given my priorities for that week. At the end of each week, I review my activities and adjust my schedule for the following week.

This level of organization might seem intense to some, but it's incredibly effective in cutting down on time-wasting and distractions. Whether you're working in a cubicle, from home, or in a busy retail environment, being intentional about how you manage your space and spend your time can lead to greater productivity and satisfaction.

Time is my most valuable resource, and wasting it is simply not an option. By being disciplined with my time—whether using my eight-sided die or the app—I achieve more and live a more fulfilling life. This approach allows me to focus on what truly matters, making the most of every moment, regardless of where I'm working.

Maximizing Every Moment

Wasting time, even in small increments, can accumulate into significant lost opportunities. Let's assess your time management skills to see how effectively you're making the most of every moment.

Ask yourself the following questions and rate yourself from 0 to 5, with 0 being "Never," 1 "Rarely," 2 "Sometimes," 3 "Often," 4 "Usually," and 5 "Always":

_____ I dedicate time weekly to strategic planning and thinking about long-term goals.

_____ I do not often waste time searching for lost or misplaced items.

_____ I am usually punctual and meet my commitments and deadlines.

_____ I rarely feel like I am forgetting something important.

_____ I rely on lists and regularly review my goals to track my progress and adjust priorities.

_____ **TOTAL**

Now, take all your numbers and add them up to get your total score. For example, if you rated yourself a four in every area, your total score would be 20. Here's how to interpret your results:

- 21 - 25: Excellent! You are an expert at managing your time and making every moment count. Keep refining your strategies to maintain this high level of efficiency.

- 16 - 20: Good work, but there's still room to optimize. Focus on areas where you scored lower to enhance your time management skills and boost productivity.

- 15 or below: Don't worry. There's always room for improvement. Start with small changes to reclaim wasted time and increase your overall productivity.

Time management isn't just about getting more done; it's about prioritizing what matters most and making deliberate choices. Here are some strategies to help you use your time more effectively:

Reflect Regularly: Dedicate a few minutes at the end of each day or week to reflect on how you spent your time. Were you focusing on activities that align with your goals and values? This reflection can help you identify areas where you might need to adjust your focus and make better use of your time.

Declutter Your Space: An organized environment reduces the time spent looking for things and minimizes distractions. Keep your workspace clean and ensure that everything has its designated place. This simple practice can save you significant time and improve your efficiency.

Prioritize Tasks Wisely: Use tools like to-do lists or digital planners to prioritize your tasks based on their importance and urgency. Start each day with the most critical tasks and work your way down the list. This approach helps you stay focused and ensures you spend your time on what truly matters.

Implementing these strategies will enhance your ability to manage time effectively and make the most of each day. Remember, it's not about doing everything but doing what counts.

Go FurtherFaster in Your Organizational Wellbeing

Organizational Wellbeing is about optimizing your environment—both personal and professional—to enhance productivity, adaptability, and overall effectiveness. It's not just about managing tasks but about cultivating a mindset that allows you to navigate life's demands with agility and purpose. This section highlighted two essential principles to boost your Organizational Wellbeing: Remain Highly Adaptable and Waste No Time.

Remain Highly Adaptable: This principle is all about embracing change and uncertainty with a positive and open mindset. In a constantly evolving world, being adaptable allows you to adjust to new situations, pivot when plans go awry, and seize unexpected opportunities. Being adaptable encourages you to stay resilient, maintain a growth mindset, and be willing to adjust your strategies to meet the moment's needs. Adaptability is not just a reaction to change; it's a proactive stance that prepares you to thrive amid uncertainty.

Waste No Time: This principle focuses on the importance of time management and the mindful use of your most precious resource—time. Not wasting time is about setting clear priorities, minimizing distractions, and planning effectively to ensure that your efforts align with your goals. By valuing your time and avoiding unnecessary activities, you can maximize productivity and create a sense of fulfillment and purpose in your daily life. This approach encourages you to live intentionally and make conscious choices that drive you toward your objectives.

Together, these principles form a dynamic duo for organizational success and personal achievement. Remaining highly adaptable ensures you are always ready to adjust to new challenges and opportunities, while wasting no time ensures that you make the most of every moment, focusing your energy where it counts the most. This combination allows you to stay agile, efficient, and aligned with your goals, both personally and professionally.

Section 6
Physical Wellbeing

Physical Wellbeing is the capacity to maintain a healthy quality of life, which enables you to maximize your participation in daily tasks, activities, work, play, and sports. This enhanced quality of life is achieved by developing strength, stamina, agility, and coordination while avoiding undue fatigue or bodily stress through adequate rest and other self-care practices [34].

Physical Wellbeing isn't just about hitting the gym or achieving a daily step count. It's about prioritizing both activity and rest that allows you to thrive in all areas of life. Focusing on physical health can often create positive changes in mental, relational, and spiritual health—and, surprisingly, even in financial health.

If you want to make a lasting change in your overall wellbeing, starting with physical health is a powerful first step. Here are two FurtherFaster Principles to consider implementing right away to enhance your Physical Wellbeing:

To Go Further: Just Stay Still

Allowing your body to rest and recover is vital for maintaining long-term physical health. Rest is a necessity that prevents injuries and combats chronic fatigue. Without adequate rest, the body cannot repair itself or prepare for future activities, leading to burnout and diminished physical capacity.

To Go Faster: Just Keep Moving

Engaging in regular physical activity provides immediate health benefits by keeping you fit and ready to tackle any task or challenge that comes your way. Staying active boosts energy levels, enhances mood, and ensures that your body is prepared for your daily demands.

In essence, achieving Physical Wellbeing requires the prioritization of both rest and activity. Rest ensures your body remains healthy and resilient over the long term, while regular activity provides the immediate fitness needed for daily life. Together, these principles create a strong foundation for thriving in all areas of life, driving positive changes beyond just physical health.

Further Principle

Just Stay Still

"Sleep is the best meditation."

- The Dalai Lama

Just staying still involves recognizing the importance of rest, sleep, and recovery as essential elements of overall wellbeing. This principle emphasizes embracing moments of stillness and taking time to pause, reflect, and rejuvenate, allowing both mind and body to recover from the demands of daily life.

Incorporating restful practices, like sleep or meditation, is vital to ensuring physical health. In fact, the National Sleep Foundation recommends that adults get 7 to 9 hours of sleep per night to support physical recovery, cognitive function, and emotional stability [36]. Even elite athletes, like NBA superstar LeBron James, understand the importance of sleep and recovery. LeBron reportedly sleeps up to 12 hours a night during the season to ensure his body and mind are fully recuperated [37].

People who embody this Just Stay Still principle appreciate the power of sleep and understand that continuous activity without periods of rest and moments of stillness can lead to burnout, decreased productivity, and poor health. By intentionally incorporating stillness into their routines—through activities like meditation, deep breathing, sitting quietly, or getting adequate rest—they're able to better manage their stress while gaining a sense of mental clarity and increased productivity.

For example, findings from Slack's Workforce Index, a survey of more than 10,000 desk workers, reveal that employees who regularly take breaks have 13% higher productivity throughout the day and report:

- 62% higher satisfaction with their work-life mix
- 43% greater ability to manage work-related stress
- 43% higher overall life satisfaction

Conversely, workers who don't take breaks are 1.7 times more likely to experience burnout [38].

These insights clearly demonstrate that incorporating periods of rest and stillness into daily life is not merely beneficial but essential. Rest allows for recovery and rejuvenation, helping individuals maintain a higher level of wellbeing and productivity.

Learning to Embrace Stillness

Growing up, I heard the phrase "Just stay still!" more times than I can count. It was hard for me—I was never one to stay still, ever. I don't remember much that my high school Spanish teacher taught me, but I do remember this over and over: *Siéntate quieto, por favor,* which translates to, "Sit still, please." At least she said please.

As an adult, I continue to struggle with the concept of stillness, but I've learned to appreciate its benefits. While staying still all day isn't my goal, intentionally embracing moments of stillness has become a valuable practice amid my often-hectic lifestyle.

For me, "staying still" might mean watching a TV show with my kids—sometimes even one I've already seen and screened to ensure it's appropriate for them. This isn't about the show itself; it's about mentally unwinding and being fully present with my children. It's a way to take a mental break and recharge.

I also get to bed a little earlier or stay in bed a bit longer after waking up. This doesn't happen often, given my active nature, but when it does, I'm not actually sleeping; I'm resting. I'm deliberately calming my muscles, mind, breathing, and emotions—either winding down at the end of the day or centering myself before facing the day ahead.

The gym is another sanctuary for me. While lifting and running are part of my routine, sometimes just going to the gym to stretch with noise-canceling headphones on is my version of "just staying still" for the week. It helps reduce tension and gives me a necessary physical and mental break.

Embracing stillness, even in small doses, has made a significant difference in my life. It's helped reduce stress, improve focus, enhance emotional wellbeing, and promote better overall physical and mental health. I don't think my childhood coaches and teachers were pushing me toward better overall wellbeing with their shouts to "stay still," but I'm grateful I learned the true benefits of stillness later in life.

Embracing the Power of Stillness

In today's fast-paced world, the concept of stillness can seem counterintuitive. However, taking time to rest and recharge is vital for maintaining your overall wellbeing. Embracing stillness allows your body and mind to recover from daily stresses, leading to better health. Let's assess how well you incorporate moments of stillness into your routine.

Ask yourself the following questions and rate yourself from 0 to 5, with 0 being "Never," 1 "Rarely," 2 "Sometimes," 3 "Often," 4 "Usually," and 5 "Always":

_____ I stretch regularly or include recovery practices (e.g., massages) in my health routine.

_____ I maintain consistent energy levels throughout the day without feeling drained.

_____ I am satisfied with the amount and quality of sleep I get each night.

_____ I regularly visit healthcare professionals or have consistent wellness checks.

_____ I take frequent breaks during my day to rest and recharge.

_____ **TOTAL**

Now, take all your numbers and add them up to get your total score. For example, if you rated yourself a four in every area, your total score would be 20. Here's how to interpret your results:

- 21 - 25: Fantastic! You are effectively incorporating stillness into your life, allowing your body and mind to recharge regularly. Keep up these great habits to maintain your wellbeing.

- 16 - 20: You're doing well, but there's room for improvement. Focus on the areas where you scored lower to enhance your ability to rest and rejuvenate.

- 15 or below: Don't worry. There are always opportunities to integrate more moments of stillness into your routine and improve your overall health.

Stillness doesn't mean being inactive; it's about giving your body and mind the opportunity to rest and rejuvenate. Here are some strategies to help you embrace stillness more effectively:

5 Minutes of Mindful Stillness: Set aside 5 minutes during your day to find a quiet spot to simply sit. Don't use your phone or any electronic devices. Just sit, let your mind wander, and enjoy the calm. This practice helps you become more comfortable with stillness and can lower stress levels.

Prioritize Quality Sleep: Establish a consistent sleep schedule by setting a regular bedtime and creating a calming bedtime routine. Consider activities such as reading, listening to soft music, or gentle stretching to wind down. Quality sleep is essential for physical and mental recovery.

Schedule Regular Breaks: Incorporate short breaks throughout your day to stretch, take a quick walk, or sit quietly. These breaks can help maintain your energy levels and improve focus, making you more productive and less stressed.

By integrating these practices into your daily routine, you'll discover stillness's benefits and feel refreshed, focused, and ready to face whatever the day brings.

Faster Principle

Just Keep Moving

"Your legs are not giving out. Your head is giving out. Keep going."

- Jillian Michaels

Just keeping moving is about incorporating regular physical activity into your daily routine to support overall health and wellbeing. This principle emphasizes the importance of consistent movement, whether through structured exercise or everyday activities, to maintain physical fitness, enhance mental clarity, and improve overall health.

A person who embodies this principle understands that movement is crucial for sustaining energy levels, enhancing mood, and supporting holistic wellbeing. They prioritize activity by integrating it into their daily routines—taking the stairs, walking during breaks, participating in sports, or even doing household chores. These individuals recognize that staying active isn't just about formal exercise sessions; it's about finding enjoyable and sustainable ways to keep moving throughout the day.

The importance of this principle is supported by compelling findings from numerous studies. For example, research analyzing publications from 2001 to 2016 revealed that sitting for more than 8 hours a day without any physical activity in that day is associated with a mortality risk comparable to that of obesity and smoking. This comprehensive analysis, which included more than one and a half million people, also found that engaging in moderate-intensity physical activity for just 60 to 75 minutes a day can mitigate the negative health effects of prolonged sitting [39]. This stark statistic underscores the critical role of regular movement in preventing life-threatening conditions. It's not just about avoiding prolonged sitting; it's about recognizing that even a small amount of physical activity can significantly impact your health outcomes.

To maximize these benefits, the US Department of Health and Human Services recommends at least 150 minutes of moderate-intensity aerobic activity or 75 minutes of vigorous-intensity aerobic activity per week, combined with muscle-strengthening activities on at least two days, to get the most health benefits out of your movement [40]. These guidelines highlight that while any type of movement is beneficial, a mix of aerobic and strength exercises offers the best outcomes for overall health and longevity. Engaging in a variety of activities supports physical health while keeping the routine fresh and engaging, making it mentally easier to maintain a consistent exercise plan.

Further emphasizing the importance of movement, a longitudinal study published in the *American Journal of Epidemiology* analyzed data from nearly 8,000 adults (ages forty-five or older in the United States) wearing an activity tracker. The study found that replacing sedentary time with physical activity significantly reduced the risk of death. Specifically, replacing 30 minutes of sitting with 30 minutes of low-intensity activity reduced the risk of early death by about 17%. More vigorous activities, like jogging or cycling, lowered the risk even further by about 35% [41]. This finding is significant—it demonstrates that every little bit of movement, no matter how small, contributes to better health and that upping the intensity of the movement yields even greater benefits. The key takeaway? You don't have to be a triathlete or a marathon runner; you just need to keep moving.

These insights clearly demonstrate that staying active is not merely a lifestyle choice but a fundamental necessity for a healthier, longer life. By making movement a regular part of your daily routine, you can boost your mood, reduce your risk of early death, improve your cardiovascular health, increase muscle strength, enhance your cognitive function, and improve your overall life satisfaction. Regular physical activity helps manage weight and reduce the risk of chronic diseases, and it also supports mental health, enhances sleep quality, and improves energy levels, ensuring you can go FurtherFaster all areas of life.

Move More, Live More

As a coach, I've guided many individuals through various physical challenges, including training for marathons. Throughout this journey, I've observed a powerful cycle of realization and transformation that occurs when people embrace movement as a core part of their lives.

Realization: The first step in this journey is realizing the significant impact that regular movement can have. When you prioritize physical activity, everything else seems to start falling into place. It's incredible how focusing on physical health—just moving more—can trigger positive changes in so many other areas of your life.

Transformation: As people commit to integrating more movement into their daily routines, a slow but steady transformation begins. It's not just about the physical changes; there's often a ripple effect. For example, they might start eating healthier naturally as their bodies crave better fuel. With more energy, they find themselves diving into hobbies and passions they once set aside. Financial health can also improve as they spend less on unnecessary things and focus on meaningful experiences. As they feel better about themselves, their relationships flourish, and they enjoy spending time with others even more.

This isn't just theory—this is real life in action. When you move more, you truly do live more. So, embrace the power of movement and let it lead you to a fuller, more vibrant life.

Energize Your Life with Movement

Physical movement is vital for maintaining your health and wellbeing. It's not just about staying fit; regular movement can boost energy, reduce stress, and enhance your overall quality of life. Let's assess how well you're incorporating movement into your daily routine.

Ask yourself the following questions and rate yourself from 0 to 5, with 0 being "Never," 1 "Rarely," 2 "Sometimes," 3 "Often," 4 "Usually," and 5 "Always":

_____ I engage in running, swimming, or cycling for at least 30 minutes three times a week.

_____ I regularly engage in strength exercises to improve muscle health and endurance.

_____ I drink plenty of caffeine-free and non-alcoholic hydrating fluids throughout my day.

_____ I track my daily movement and aim for regular intervals of activity, such as walking.

_____ I intentionally choose activities that require physical movement, like taking stairs.

_____ **TOTAL**

Now, take all your numbers and add them up to get your total score. For example, if you rated yourself a four in every area, your total score would be 20. Here's how to interpret your results:

- 21 - 25: Fantastic! You're making movement a priority in your life. Keep nurturing these habits to maintain your health and vitality.

- 16 - 20: You're doing well, but there's room for improvement. Focus on areas where you scored lower to boost your activity levels.

- 15 or below: Don't worry. It's never too late to start incorporating more movement into your day.

Physical activity doesn't have to be strenuous or time-consuming. Here are three practical steps to help you stay active:

Add Movement to Your Routine: Keep your walking shoes near your most-used door as a visual reminder to take short walks throughout the day. Even a few minutes of walking can help you reach the recommended 10,000 steps daily.

Hydration and Recovery: Stay hydrated throughout the day to maintain your energy levels. Aim to drink about 3.7 liters (125 ounces) for men and 2.7 liters (91 ounces) for women, as recommended by the National Academies. According to the Institute of Medicine of the National Academies of Sciences, proper hydration is essential for both physical performance and recovery.

Strength Training Integration: Incorporate simple strength training exercises into your daily routine, such as squats, push-ups, or resistance band exercises. You can do these while watching TV or waiting for the coffee to boil. Regular strength training improves muscle strength, bone density, and overall metabolism.

By focusing on these key actions, you'll increase your physical activity and improve your overall health and wellbeing.

Go FurtherFaster in Your Physical Wellbeing

Physical Wellbeing is the cornerstone of a healthy, vibrant life. It's about more than just fitness; it's about creating a routine that includes both movement and rest to maintain your body in its best condition. In this section, we explored two essential principles to enhance Physical Wellbeing: Just Stay Still and Just Keep Moving.

Just Stay Still: This principle underscores the vital role of rest and recovery in maintaining overall health. In our fast-paced world, it's easy to overlook the power of stillness, but taking time to relax, sleep adequately, and engage in restorative practices is essential for preventing burnout and maintaining physical and mental resilience. Practicing these practices reminds us that stillness is not a sign of inactivity but a necessary part of recharging our bodies and minds. Embracing rest helps reduce stress, improve concentration, and support recovery, enabling you to perform at your best.

Just Keep Moving: This principle advocates for integrating regular physical activity into your daily routine. Movement isn't limited to intense workouts or structured exercise; it's about staying active in ways that fit naturally into your life, like walking, gardening, or stretching. Embracing physical activity encourages you to move frequently to maintain fitness, boost energy levels, and enhance overall wellbeing. Regular activity helps improve cardiovascular health, strengthen muscles, and boost mood, providing a solid foundation for a healthy lifestyle.

Together, these principles create a holistic approach to physical health, ensuring that you have the energy to go FurtherFaster in all aspects of your life!

Section 7
Recreational Wellbeing

Recreational Wellbeing involves engaging in activities or pursuits during discretionary time—time free from personal and professional obligations—that enhance the quality of your life. These activities satisfy either basic needs (such as safety, health, or sensory enjoyment) or growth needs (like aesthetic appreciation, moral development, or mastery of a skill) and have been proven to lower depression, improve physical health, foster personal growth, and even build social connections [42].

In addition, these types of recreational activities allow us to escape from daily stress, sharpen our skills, stretch ourselves beyond our comfort zones, and enjoy life more fully.

As with many of the FurtherFaster Principles, it's important to prioritize these opposite yet complementary forces. Let's explore the following FurtherFaster Principles to enhance your Recreational Wellbeing so you can create momentum and promote long-term growth.

To Go Further: Finish Something Hard

Engaging in challenging recreational activities builds resilience and promotes long-term personal growth. These activities push your boundaries and reveal your capacity for transformation and deeper change. To truly go further, challenge yourself and finish something hard.

To Go Faster: Make It Easy

By choosing activities that are easy to start and enjoy, you create immediate positive experiences that give you a sense of accomplishment and motivate you to continue. This approach helps you stay engaged in the short-term and encourages you to stick with your recreational pursuits for the rest of your life.

Further Principle

Finish Something Hard

"Success isn't always about greatness; it's about consistency. Consistent, hard work gains success."

- Dwayne Johnson

Finishing something hard means embracing challenges that require effort, perseverance, and resilience, ultimately leading to transformative change. It involves taking on difficult tasks—whether physical, mental, or emotional—and committing to seeing them through to the end. This principle is about building endurance and strength over time, pushing yourself to grow in ways that simpler tasks cannot achieve.

A person who embodies this principle approaches difficult tasks with determination and a growth mindset. They understand that long-term success requires facing challenges head-on and that growth happens outside their comfort zone. By consistently finishing hard things, they build resilience and adaptability—traits essential for navigating the uncertainties of life.

Research supports this approach. For example, experts in goal-setting theory have demonstrated that people who set "challenging goals" are 90% more likely to achieve their desired outcomes than those who set more "manageable" or "do your best" goals [43]. Also, a study published in the *European Journal of Investigation in Health, Psychology, and Education* found that individuals who engage in physically demanding activities, such as mountain climbing or marathon running, report higher levels of self-efficacy, self-esteem, and overall life satisfaction [44].

This research also mirrors what I've seen in the faces of people I coach: Once they complete a seemingly unattainable goal, like running a marathon, they realize their own strength and potential. They think, "If I can do that, I can do anything."

It's like how James Clear, in his best-selling book *Atomic Habits*, emphasizes the importance of embracing difficulty and discomfort for personal growth. He states, "Exercising is easier once you've started the workout. Conversation is easier once you're already talking. Writing is easier once you're in the middle of it. But many rewards in life will elude you if you're not willing to be a little uncomfortable at first" [45].

These studies, statistics, and insights clearly show that consistently engaging in and finishing hard tasks builds resilience, develops a deeper appreciation for your abilities, and increases your confidence to propel you to further success in all areas of life.

Crossing the Finish Line of Life's Challenges

I've always been drawn to challenges, and triathlons are one of my favorite ways to push my limits. Training for and competing in a triathlon is far from easy, especially when you push yourself to the edge of your physical and mental capacities. But the rewards of finishing are immense, far beyond the race itself.

For example, when I challenge myself in training or on the course, the benefits extend to all areas of my life. The discipline and perseverance required to prepare for and complete a triathlon give me the strength to tackle work projects, public speaking, and personal challenges with renewed determination and confidence. Each time I push myself in one area of life, I find myself thinking, "If I can do that, what else am I capable of?"

One particular half marathon stands out in my memory when I was running alongside a buddy of mine. Physically, I felt strong. But mentally, I was ready to quit. Thoughts like, "Why am I out here? Why am I pushing myself this hard?" kept creeping into my mind. On the other hand, my buddy's mental resolve was rock-solid. But his body was telling him to slow down.

As we neared the finish line, I kept our pace steady while he spoke words of encouragement to keep us going. My physical strength and his mental fortitude carried us both through to the finish line, allowing us to finish strong and achieve a time faster than either of us thought possible.

What did completing this hard challenge teach us? I realized my mind could endure more than I believed, and he discovered his body was stronger than he had ever imagined. We both learned a valuable lesson that day: We are capable of far more than we give ourselves credit for. Crossing that finish line was not just about completing a race; it was about proving to ourselves that we could overcome obstacles and achieve our goals.

Taking on Hard Tasks

Taking on and finishing hard challenges builds resilience and reveals untapped strengths, helping you grow in ways you never thought possible. Let's assess how well you take on hard tasks.

Ask yourself the following questions and rate yourself from 0 to 5, with 0 being "Never," 1 "Rarely," 2 "Sometimes," 3 "Often," 4 "Usually," and 5 "Always":

_____ I seek out recreational activities that stretch my limits and encourage personal growth.

_____ I intentionally pursue goals that require sustained effort and perseverance.

_____ I finished something hard within the past month.

_____ I seek out recreational activities that push me out of my comfort zone.

____ I follow a consistent schedule to complete challenging recreational tasks.

____ **TOTAL**

Now, take all your numbers and add them up to get your total score. For example, if you rated yourself a four in every area, your total score would be 20. Here's how to interpret your results:

- 21 - 25: Excellent! You are not afraid to take on hard tasks and push yourself beyond your comfort zone. Keep challenging yourself to grow even more.

- 16 - 20: Good job, but there's room for improvement. Focus on areas where you scored lower to embrace more challenging tasks and nurture personal growth.

- 15 or below: Don't worry. It's never too late to start taking on more challenging activities to build resilience and confidence.

Taking on difficult tasks can be intimidating, but it's also incredibly rewarding. Here are three steps to help you get started with and finish something hard:

Set a Bold Goal: Identify a challenging yet exciting goal—like running a marathon, learning a new skill, or completing a complex project. Break it down into smaller, manageable steps and create a plan to tackle each step consistently.

Incorporate Daily Challenges: Challenge yourself in small ways every day. It could be taking a cold shower, reading a complex book, or tackling a new workout routine. These daily challenges build mental toughness and prepare you for bigger tasks.

Reflect and Learn: Take time to reflect on the challenges you've faced and the progress you've made. Celebrate your successes, learn from any setbacks, and use these experiences as motivation to take on new, harder challenges.

By consistently taking on and finishing hard tasks, you'll develop greater resilience, confidence, and personal growth, giving you the mental fortitude you need to tackle anything life throws your way.

Faster Principle

Make It Easy

"Life is really simple, but we insist on making it complicated."

- Confucius

Making it easy revolves around engaging in simple, enjoyable activities that are immediately gratifying and fit seamlessly into your daily routine. The essence of this principle is not about avoiding all challenges; it's about finding a happy medium between effort and ease, ensuring that your recreational pursuits remain a source of joy and satisfaction. To Make It Easy, you prioritize activities that require minimal effort and preparation, allowing you to quickly slip into a state of enjoyment and relaxation. The goal is to build momentum and confidence by achieving quick wins through easy, accessible recreational activities.

For instance, consider the act of reading—a seemingly effortless activity. Research from the University of Sussex shows that reading for just 6 minutes can lower stress levels by up to 68% [46].

And it gets even better because it doesn't matter if you choose reading, gardening, cooking, fishing, walking, or playing board games. Choosing activities that require minimal effort but provide maximum enjoyment can be a powerful tool for maintaining health in life. The key, however, is to find what works for you and to make it a consistent part of your wellbeing regimen.

Keep It Simple, Keep It Fun

My journey with music began early, thanks to my parents. At age five, they started me on piano lessons. By thirteen, I was eager for a change and chose to learn the drums—naturally, an exciting shift for any teenager. Not long after, my grandfather gifted me a guitar along with a book and record titled "Teach Yourself to Play Guitar." That was the turning point. I was instantly hooked. I realized my right hand, trained from playing the drums, was perfect for strumming, while my left hand, skilled from the piano, was suited for the fretboard. The guitar felt easy, almost intuitive, and I never looked back.

While mastering the piano and coordinating my limbs on the drums was challenging at first, picking up the guitar felt natural. Over the years, I've taken lessons and learned more advanced techniques, but the guitar has always remained my go-to. Now, decades later, I have a guitar next to me in my office, and I play it weekly as the worship leader at my church. It's more than just a hobby; it's become a fun, social, and fulfilling way to give back to my community.

When you choose recreational activities that are easy to integrate into your life and that you genuinely enjoy, you're much more likely to stick with them. Too often, people start hobbies that frustrate them or feel overly complicated. While some things worth doing are challenging, it's important to have activities that provide quick satisfaction and are simple to engage in regularly. If an activity becomes too frustrating, it's okay to pivot and find something that feels more natural and enjoyable.

After all, by keeping it simple and fun, you're more likely to maintain your enthusiasm and commitment, leading to a more vibrant and fulfilling life. Engaging in easy, pleasurable activities reduces stress, improves mood, and promotes a sense of relaxation and joy.

Finding Joy in Simple Pleasures

Engaging in recreational activities that you enjoy is vital for your mental health and overall wellbeing. It's about finding simple pleasures that bring joy and even relaxation to your life. Let's see how well you're doing in this area.

Ask yourself the following questions and rate yourself from 0 to 5, with 0 being "Never," 1 "Rarely," 2 "Sometimes," 3 "Often," 4 "Usually," and 5 "Always":

_____ I make time for low-effort recreational activities to unwind and experience simple joys.

_____ I make time for fun, low-effort activities that help me relax.

_____ I consistently include simple activities like crafts, gardening, or walking into my routine.

_____ I take short breaks throughout the day to engage in enjoyable, low-effort activities.

_____ I participate in easy, fun activities with family or friends to enhance my relationships.

_____ **TOTAL**

Now, take all your numbers and add them up to get your total score. For example, if you rated yourself a four in every area, your total score would be 20. Here's how to interpret your results:

- 21 - 25: Fantastic! You are effectively incorporating enjoyable activities into your life. Keep nurturing these habits to feel fulfilled.

- 16 - 20: You're doing well, but there's room for improvement. Focus on areas where you scored lower to bring more joy and relaxation into your routine.

- 15 or below: Don't worry. It's never too late to start incorporating more fun and relaxing activities into your life.

Making time for recreational activities doesn't have to be complicated. Here are three steps to help you easily integrate joy into your life:

Discover Your Passions: Make a list of activities that interest you or you've always thought you'd enjoy or be good at. Whether painting, gardening, hiking, or learning a new language, start exploring to find what truly brings you joy.

Prioritize "Me Time": Schedule dedicated time each week for your chosen activities. Treat this time as a priority—just as important as work meetings or other obligations. Consistent "me time" helps reduce stress and enhances your overall wellbeing.

Connect with Like-Minded People: Join a club, class, or online group that shares your interests. Engaging with others who have similar passions can provide motivation, create a sense of community, and make the activity more enjoyable.

By taking these steps, you'll create more space in your life for activities that bring joy and fulfillment, enhancing your overall wellbeing.

Go FurtherFaster in Your Recreational Wellbeing

Recreational Wellbeing is a vital component of a healthy life. It involves finding joy, relaxation, and fulfillment in activities that recharge your spirit and enrich your daily experience. In this section, we explored two key principles to boost Recreational Wellbeing: Finish Something Hard and Make It Easy.

Finish Something Hard: This principle focuses on the importance of embracing challenges that require effort, perseverance, and resilience. Taking on something challenging encourages you to step out of your comfort zone to engage in activities that stretch your abilities, whether it's mastering a new skill, completing a challenging project, or achieving a physical feat. By finishing hard tasks, you build resilience, enhance your problem-solving skills, and gain a deep sense of accomplishment. These experiences promote personal growth and boost confidence, helping you realize your potential over the long term.

Make It Easy: This principle emphasizes the value of integrating simple, enjoyable activities into your routine for quick, achievable wins. Engaging in simple activities you enjoy helps you discover hobbies or interests that bring you joy and encourages you to make time for them regularly. Engaging in easy, fun activities isn't about avoiding all challenges; it's about creating accessible opportunities for relaxation and pleasure. These activities provide immediate satisfaction and serve as a refreshing break from the demands of daily life, helping to reduce stress and enhance your overall quality of life.

The synergy between these two principles is key to Recreational Wellbeing. Finish Something Hard helps you build long-term resilience and personal growth, while Make It Easy provides the immediate satisfaction and motivation needed to keep you engaged.

By incorporating both easy and challenging activities into your life, you can enjoy a well-rounded recreational experience that nourishes your body, mind, and spirit, allowing you to go FurtherFaster in all aspects of your life.

Section 8
Relational Wellbeing

Relational Wellbeing refers to the quality of interpersonal interactions that are positive, growth-fostering, supportive, mutually empathic, and empowering. This encompasses relationships with family, friends, and the community, as well as within organizational and geographic spheres.

But what happens if we don't actively cultivate our relationships? If we allow them to fester or fail to seek them out intentionally, we risk emotional isolation, stagnation, and increased stress. Relationships are the bedrock of our social existence, and neglecting them can lead to a diminished sense of belonging and support.

To guide you in enhancing your Relational Wellbeing, consider these FurtherFaster Principles:

To Go Further: Love Your People

Developing deep, meaningful relationships provides lasting support, comfort, and happiness. These connections are your anchor in challenging times, offering stability and emotional security. Without them, you risk feeling isolated and unsupported, missing out on the deep fulfillment that comes from being truly connected with others.

To Go Faster: Find New Friends

Expanding your social circle introduces immediate companionship, joy, and opportunities for growth. Building friendships can bring fresh perspectives, new hobbies, career opportunities, and a broader social network. Without actively seeking new connections, you may never experience the engagement and vibrancy of a diverse social circle.

Prioritizing deep, meaningful relationships and expanding your social network ensures Relational Wellbeing. Embrace both principles to build a fulfilling and resilient social life.

Further Principle

Love Your People

"We are biologically, cognitively, physically, and spiritually wired to love, to be loved, and to belong."

- Brené Brown

Loving your people involves investing deeply in meaningful, supportive relationships that provide emotional sustenance and a sense of belonging. You see, it's not about having a large number of acquaintances. It's about nurturing a few key relationships that truly matter—whether they are with family, close friends, or significant others.

These deep, genuine connections are built on trust, empathy, and mutual respect. They form a solid foundation for Relational Wellbeing that provides us with a sense of security and support, sustains us through both joyful moments and hardships, and enhances our physical health and emotional wellbeing.

And this isn't just my opinion. Research supports the critical importance of these few deep connections. According to The American Psychological Association, close, meaningful relationships help reduce stress, boost immune function, and even increase life expectancy. Also, according to Holt-Lunstad, Smith, and Layton, people with strong social relationships are 50% less likely to die prematurely compared to those with weaker social ties [47].

All this to say, having a few deep, meaningful relationships is beneficial for a healthy and fulfilling life, and these relationships strengthen resilience, provide unwavering support, and enrich our lives in countless ways.

Cherishing Deep Connections

I often exercise on a trail around a park near my home. During peak times, the park is filled with people, including many older, retired couples walking hand-in-hand. Moving slowly and carefully, some of these couples radiate a sense of peace and fulfillment. They shuffle along the granite path, supporting one another and engaging in quiet, meaningful conversations.

Every time I see them, I think to myself, "That will be my wife and me someday." This thought is both comforting and inspiring. It serves as a powerful reminder of the importance of cultivating deep, meaningful relationships throughout our lives. Having someone to share our journey with—someone who truly knows us and loves us unconditionally—allows us to be our authentic selves and experience the joy of loving and being loved.

A poignant example of this in my life was my relationship with my dad. We were incredibly close, and I used to call him every day on my drive home from work. We'd talk about work, family, and the ups and downs of life. His passing from cancer was devastating, leaving a huge void in my heart. I still miss those daily conversations and the deep bond we shared. While my sons never had the opportunity to know him as I did, I hope to pass on his love through my actions and words to them. The love I received from my dad and continue to receive from my mom has shaped who I am and how I love others.

Loving some people deeply enriches our lives in ways that nothing else can. It provides us with strength, support, and a sense of belonging. These relationships—whether with family, friends, or a life partner—are what make life truly meaningful and fulfilling. They remind us that love is the greatest gift we can give and receive, even in life's quiet, ordinary moments.

Loving Others More

Building and nurturing deep relationships is essential for your emotional wellbeing. It's about cultivating meaningful connections where love is both given and received in enriching ways. Let's assess how well you're fostering these loving relationships.

Ask yourself the following questions and rate yourself from 0 to 5, with 0 being "Never," 1 "Rarely," 2 "Sometimes," 3 "Often," 4 "Usually," and 5 "Always":

_____ I regularly provide emotional support and encouragement to my family or close friends.

_____ I take time to benefit from and enjoy my family or close friends.

_____ I have at least one close relationship I feel is unconditional.

_____ I use my creativity to solve problems or bring joy to my close relationships.

_____ I resolve conflicts in a positive and respectful manner.

_____ **TOTAL**

Now, take all your numbers and add them up to get your total score. For example, if you rated yourself a four in every area, your total score would be 20. Here's how to interpret your results:

- 21 - 25: Wonderful! You are deeply invested in fostering loving relationships. Keep nurturing these connections to maintain and enhance your emotional well-being.

- 16 - 20: You're doing well, but there's room for improvement. Focus on areas where you scored lower to deepen your relationships further.

- 15 or below: Don't worry. It's never too late to build stronger, more loving relationships with those around you.

Loving others isn't about grand gestures; the small, everyday actions truly show you care. Here are three steps to help you love some people more deeply:

Prioritize Quality Time: Make it a point to spend quality time with a loved one each week. Whether it's a family member, friend, or partner, engage in activities you both enjoy and focus on genuinely connecting.

Practice Acts of Kindness: Perform small, meaningful acts of kindness for the people you love. This could be cooking their favorite meal, writing a heartfelt note, or simply being a good listener. These gestures can strengthen your bonds significantly.

Enhance Communication: Foster open and honest communication with your loved ones. Share your thoughts and feelings, and encourage them to do the same. Building trust through communication strengthens your connection and deepens your relationships.

Focusing on these steps will help you build stronger, more loving relationships and create a more supportive and emotionally enriching environment for yourself and others.

Faster Principle

Find New Friends

"You are my friend. You are special. You are my friend. You're special to me."

- Fred Rogers

Friendships are fundamental to emotional support, shared experiences, and overall wellbeing. Finding friends goes beyond simply meeting new people; it's about actively cultivating a wide network of social connections that bring joy, companionship, and a sense of community into your life. Having a diverse group of friends can take you faster in life, supporting your personal and professional growth in ways that few other resources can.

A person who embodies the principle actively seeks out opportunities to build relationships—whether by attending social events, joining clubs or groups of interest, or simply engaging with new people. Building and nurturing friendships requires time and effort, but the rewards—emotional support, shared joy, and a sense of belonging—are invaluable.

A diverse group of friends exposes us to new ideas, different perspectives, and varied activities, which can broaden our horizons and drive personal growth. The Harvard Study of Adult Development, one of the longest-running studies on human happiness, found that the key to living a happy and fulfilling life isn't wealth or fame but having strong relationships and engaging in meaningful activities [48]. This finding reinforces the idea that cultivating a wide range of friendships is essential for personal wellbeing and professional effectiveness.

In today's society, finding friendships in the workplace has become increasingly important. The Harvard Study again noted that "Americans are now more likely to make friends at work than in any other setting, including school, neighborhood, or places of worship" [49]. This shift suggests that cultivating friendships in professional environments is essential for career development and job satisfaction. Networking through friendships can lead to job opportunities, collaborations, and professional growth, as many jobs are now found through social connections rather than traditional job postings.

Additionally, maintaining a large social circle can positively impact your physical health. According to research by Holt-Lunstad, Smith, and Layton, people with strong social connections are 50% more likely to thrive than those with weaker relationships [50]. Having a broad network of friends helps reduce stress, encourages healthier lifestyle choices, and creates a sense of belonging, all contributing to improved overall health and longevity.

In conclusion, a large network of friends keeps you engaged, provides diverse support, introduces you to new experiences, and nurtures both personal and professional growth. Whether you're seeking new connections or strengthening existing ones, the effort invested in friendships is always worthwhile.

Building Bonds Over Brisket

Whenever I'm in a social setting with my wife and we have to introduce ourselves, she often tells others jokingly that I have more pairs of shoes than she does. It's true—I have running shoes, church shoes, camping boots, house shoes, worship-leading shoes, beach shoes, work shoes, biking shoes, and more. Each pair is a metaphor for a different aspect of my life, each connecting me to a diverse network of friends and communities.

These multiple social circles have significantly impacted my life. Most of my new opportunities, whether extra game tickets, dinner invitations, job offers, or unexpected adventures, come from friends within these networks. Having a wide, dynamic network of friends and acquaintances keeps life vibrant and full of possibilities.

One of the most rewarding social circles I belong to is our church worship team. Although we meet twice a week— once for practice and once for the service—it's often difficult to get to know everyone well during those busy times. Between rehearsals and the pressures of Sunday mornings, there's little time to connect beyond the music. Plus, with rotating musicians and volunteers filling in from time to time, it's easy to miss out on the opportunity to build relationships.

That's why I host a "meeat night" every few months at my house. We "meet" over "meat." The team brings sides and desserts, and I smoke brisket, ribs, salmon, and more. It's a laid-back evening that gives everyone a way to meet each other beyond the formality of church roles. Instead of just practicing together, we talk about our families, work, hobbies, and even those little challenges we all face—whether it's fixing a car or balancing a tough decision. Newer members get an opportunity to introduce themselves, and we all expand our social network.

These nights are about multiplying our connections and getting to know each other in ways that deepen our musical collaboration while helping our social network grow. Some people who may have never spoken at length during practice find common ground and new friendships. The connections formed during these nights ripple out into the broader community, strengthening both our personal lives and our music as a collective.

Hosting "meeat night" is more than just a social event—the relationships we form during these kinds of gatherings enrich our lives in unexpected ways, opening up new possibilities and strengthening our connections to others.

Building a Strong Social Circle

Having a solid social network is vital for your emotional and mental wellbeing. It's not just about meeting new people; it's about building and maintaining meaningful friendships that provide support, companionship, and joy. Let's see how well you're doing in this area.

Ask yourself the following questions and rate yourself from 0 to 5, with 0 being "Never," 1 "Rarely," 2 "Sometimes," 3 "Often," 4 "Usually," and 5 "Always":

_____ I have a set of friends I communicate with outside of social media.

_____ I am not involved in any abusive or toxic relationships.

_____ I belong to a group, club, or committee with many members.

_____ I have good relationships with my coworkers, co-volunteers, and peers.

_____ I seek out new relationships and take time to net work.

_____ **TOTAL**

Now, take all your numbers and add them up to get your total score. For example, if you rated yourself a four in every area, your total score would be 20. Here's how to interpret your results:

- 21 - 25: Excellent! You have a strong social network and meaningful friendships. Keep nurturing these connections to maintain a supportive community around you.

- 16 - 20: Good effort, but there's room for growth. Focus on areas where you scored lower to strengthen and expand your social circle.

- 15 or below: Don't worry. It's never too late to build and strengthen your network of friends and acquaintances.

Building friendships isn't just about meeting new people; it's about creating meaningful, lasting connections. Here are three steps to help you find and nurture friendships:

Join a Community: Find a local group or club that aligns with your interests. Whether it's a sports team, book club, or volunteer organization, participating in group activities can help you meet new people and form lasting bonds.

Reach Out Regularly: Make a conscious effort to reach out to someone new or reconnect with someone you've lost touch with each week. Start a conversation, grab a coffee, or simply check in. Building relationships requires consistent effort.

Strengthen Existing Bonds: Dedicate time to nurturing your friendships. Plan regular meetups, phone calls, or video chats, and be proactive in showing your appreciation and support for your friends.

By following these steps, you'll cultivate a vibrant social network, enriching your life with diverse connections and friendships.

Go FurtherFaster in Your Relational Wellbeing

Relational Wellbeing is at the heart of a fulfilling life. It involves cultivating meaningful connections and maintaining a supportive network of relationships that provide both emotional sustenance and joy. In this section, we focused on two foundational principles to enhance Relational Wellbeing: Love Your People and Find New Friends.

Love Your People: This principle is about investing deeply in close, unconditional relationships. Fostering deep relationships encourages you to prioritize quality over quantity, focusing on nurturing bonds with those who matter most. These deep relationships serve as a reliable source of emotional support, helping you navigate life's ups and downs with a sense of security and belonging. When you love deeply, you enrich the lives of those you care about and also your own, strengthening a sense of connection and fulfillment.

Find New Friends: This principle underscores the importance of expanding your social network and engaging with new people. Meeting new people highlights the value of forming diverse friendships that bring different perspectives and experiences into your life. Building a wide-ranging social circle provides companionship and fun and offers opportunities for personal growth, collaboration, and learning. Whether through shared activities, common interests, or professional networking, forming new connections keeps your social life dynamic and stimulating, enriching your personal and professional spheres.

Rather than seeing these approaches as opposites, consider them complementary strategies that together form a full and rewarding relational experience. By nurturing both deep bonds and expanding your social network, you can create a rich tapestry of connections that support, challenge, and fulfill you throughout your life—enabling you to go FurtherFaster in your journey toward a life filled with love, companionship, and meaningful connection.

Section 9
Spiritual Wellbeing

Spiritual Wellbeing involves our satisfaction with the search for deeper meaning in life through the integration of self-purpose. For many, this pertains to a belief in and connectedness to a higher power—be it God, Allah, Brahma, Vishnu, Shiva, Buddha, Yahweh, another divine entity, humanity, nature, or the universe.

Research consistently shows that humans derive profound satisfaction from the quest for deeper meaning and interconnectedness. This pursuit, often referred to as self-purpose, involves looking beyond the mundane aspects of daily life to seek an understanding of who we are and what we stand for.

This sense of purpose can be cultivated through religious practices, meditation, spending time in nature, or simple acts of kindness and compassion toward others.

To cultivate Spiritual Wellbeing, consider these Further-Faster Principles:

To Go Further: Listen to Truth

Seeking and adhering to deeper truths provides a foundation for lasting spiritual growth. Without this commitment, one's spiritual journey may become shallow and unfulfilled.

To Go Faster: Learn with Purpose

Engaging in purposeful learning and experiences accelerates your spiritual journey. Without intentional focus, you may bounce aimlessly from one thing to another.

You nurture lasting spiritual growth by grounding yourself in deeper truths, while purposeful learning and experiences rapidly enhance your spiritual journey. Embrace both to go FurtherFaster in your Spiritual Wellbeing.

Further Principle

Listen to Truth

"Then you will know the truth, and the truth will set you free."

- John 8:32 (NIV Bible)

Listening to truth involves actively seeking deeper understanding that aligns with our core values and beliefs, guiding our actions and decisions. It's about maintaining openness to new insights and perspectives, even when they challenge our existing beliefs or comfort zones. Embracing truth in all its forms fosters personal growth, self-awareness, and spiritual development.

Truth has a transformative power that brings clarity and understanding to our lives. When we genuinely seek the truth, we become better equipped to make informed decisions that align with our values. This alignment cultivates a sense of authenticity, enabling us to live with integrity and purpose. Those who embody this principle are committed to honesty and integrity, pursuing truth with an open mind and a willingness to confront uncomfortable realities. By doing so, they empower themselves to grow both personally and spiritually.

Research supports the importance of nurturing a spiritual aspect in life. A study found that individuals who maintained a spiritual practice, such as self-reflection, prayer, meditation, or service, were less likely to experience depression over time. This suggests that connecting with a higher truth—however one defines it—offers significant mental health benefits and emotional resilience [52].

Another recent study further finds that having a strong sense of purpose in life is associated with a lower risk of death from any cause, applicable across various demographics, including race, ethnicity, and gender. This study assessed more than 13,000 people and found that those with the highest sense of purpose and truth had a significantly lower risk of death compared to those with the lowest sense of purpose, emphasizing that cultivating a spiritual life is as impactful for longevity as maintaining physical health [53].

In the professional realm, maintaining a strong moral compass and adhering to personal principles can significantly impact career success and life satisfaction. Individuals who stay true to their values are more likely to achieve their goals and report higher levels of fulfillment. This commitment to integrity and truth can lead to greater professional advancement, as staying true to one's values is often associated with higher rates of promotion and career success [54].

These findings clearly demonstrate that listening to truth and cultivating some form of spiritual life—whether through religion, meditation, or a personal belief system—is essential for overall wellbeing.

Guided by a Personal Compass

Having a core belief system rooted in my faith in Jesus, God, and the Holy Spirit has never steered me wrong in life. It's like having a personal compass that guides my decisions, especially during tough times. I pray daily, attempt to read the Bible with regularity, and follow the principles laid out therein. This belief system has provided me with a firm foundation—something I can always rely on when facing important decisions or navigating new opportunities.

One specific moment where this came into play was during a major business decision. I had two choices: work with a former employer who was a "sure thing" but didn't quite align with my values or take a leap and partner with someone new who perfectly resonated with my Christian beliefs. The former was financially attractive, but the latter felt right spiritually. I chose the new partner because the decision aligned with my faith. To my surprise, this led to immense personal and professional growth and resulted in a much larger financial gain than I could have ever anticipated.

That experience is just one example. I have countless others involving personal relationships, finances, and more—

where trusting in God's principles, as laid out in the Bible, has improved my wellbeing and led to tangible blessings. The community I've built through my church, the strengthening of familial ties, and the immense peace I've found in my daily walk with God have all enhanced my life in ways that can't always be measured by external success but by a deep, internal sense of fulfillment and purpose.

Aligning with Your Core Truths

Listening to truth involves being open to honest feedback, understanding your core values, and making choices that align with those values. It's about actively seeking the truth in yourself and the world around you and letting it guide your decisions and actions. Let's see how well you're integrating this principle into your life.

Ask yourself the following questions and rate yourself from 0 to 5, with 0 being "Never," 1 "Rarely," 2 "Sometimes," 3 "Often," 4 "Usually," and 5 "Always":

____ I can discuss my own death with family and friends openly.

____ I spend a portion of every day in prayer, meditation, or personal reflection.

____ I engage in activities like reflection, study, or service to deepen my spiritual connection.

____ I experience a sense of connection with a higher power, nature, or the transcendent.

_____ I maintain a consistent sense of spiritual connection during routine moments.

_____ **TOTAL**

Now, take all your numbers and add them up to get your total score. For example, if you rated yourself a four in every area, your total score would be 20. Here's how to interpret your results:

- 21 - 25: Fantastic! You have a strong alignment with your core truths and values. Keep nurturing this awareness to connect deeply with yourself and the world.

- 16 - 20: You're on the right path, but there's room for deepening your connection. Consider focusing on areas where you scored lower to enhance your alignment with truth.

- 15 or below: Don't worry. It's a journey, and you can start building a stronger connection to your core truths anytime.

Aligning with your core truths isn't just about introspection; it's about living out your values daily. Here are three steps to help you connect more deeply with the truth:

Daily Reflection Practice: Dedicate time each day to prayer, meditation, or personal reflection. This quiet time allows you to connect with your inner self, understand your core values, and assess how well your actions align with them.

Seek Honest Feedback: Invite trusted friends, mentors, or family members to provide you with honest feedback about your actions and choices. Be open to their perspectives, and use their insights to refine your approach to life and align more closely with your values.

Reconnect with Nature: Spend time outdoors, whether it's a walk in the park, a hike in the mountains, or just sitting in your backyard. Nature can offer a sense of grounding and clarity, helping you feel more connected to the world and more aware of your place within it.

Integrating these practices into your daily routine will enhance your ability to listen to truth and align your actions with your deepest values, leading to a more authentic and fulfilling life.

Faster Principle

Learn with Purpose

"The more that you read, the more things you will know. The more that you learn, the more places you'll go."

- Dr. Seuss

Learning with purpose involves engaging in educational pursuits that are closely aligned with your values, passions, and long-term goals. This approach goes beyond simply acquiring knowledge; it's about seeking meaningful and relevant learning experiences that contribute to personal and professional development. When we learn with intention, education transforms from a passive activity into an active, engaged journey toward growth and fulfillment.

A person who embodies this principle intentionally focuses on their learning journey. They carefully select subjects and skills that resonate with their aspirations, ensuring their educational efforts are both directed and purposeful. This approach to learning grows intrinsic motivation, as it aligns with what truly matters to the individual, making the learning process more engaging and fulfilling.

Research supports the numerous benefits of purposeful learning. For example, studies indicate that students who follow a more individualized and purpose-driven educational approach, such as homeschooling, tend to perform better academically. Homeschooled students typically score 15 to 30 percentile points higher on standardized tests than their public-school peers, suggesting that a clear purpose and personalized learning plan can significantly enhance academic outcomes [55].

Beyond academic success, purposeful learning also contributes to better mental and physical health. A study published in *Psychosomatic Medicine* found that older adults with a higher sense of purpose were less likely to experience cognitive decline, Alzheimer's disease, or functional deterioration. This study showed that those with a well-defined life purpose had a 30% lower risk of cognitive decline and mortality, highlighting the importance of engaging in purposeful activities for strengthening resilience and promoting longevity [56].

Learning with purpose is a lifelong journey that enhances intellectual development and promotes emotional and spiritual fulfillment. By aligning educational endeavors with personal passions and goals, individuals can create a rich, rewarding life filled with continuous growth and meaningful contributions. This approach encourages us to engage deeply with the world around us, fostering a sense of purpose and connection that enriches both our personal and professional lives.

Crafting a Purposeful Legacy

I've always believed in learning and leading with a clear purpose, but this belief became especially strong during my PhD program in emotional intelligence. During one of our sessions, my mentor gave me an unusual assignment: to write a eulogy speech—not for someone else, but for myself. He wanted me to imagine it was decades in the future and that my son was standing up at my funeral to read it. "My dad…" he would begin. But what would he say next? What did I truly want him to say?

I wrote what I thought was a heartfelt and inspiring eulogy and turned it in, feeling confident about my work. Not long after, I received it back with a note from my mentor: *This is what everyone wants their son to say about them. What do you, personally, really want him to say? Rewrite and return.*

This feedback prompted deeper reflection. I spent much more time thinking about what truly mattered to me, what kind of man and father I wanted to be remembered as, and how I wanted to impact my son's life. I rewrote the eulogy, this time infusing it with genuine personal desires and aspirations. When I turned it in, my mentor gave me a glowing review. However, I realized that the man I described in that eulogy was not who I was at that moment—yet.

That exercise gave me a clear vision of who I wanted to become. It gave me a sense of purpose and direction for my learning and growth. From then on, I started actively seeking experiences, knowledge, and skills to help me become the person I envisioned in that eulogy. I began to live out the FurtherFaster principle of "learn with purpose."

This purposeful approach to learning has been transformative. It's not just about acquiring knowledge; it's about intentional growth and development. Every book I read, course I take, and experience I seek out is now aligned with my goal of becoming the person I want to be. So, who do you want to be? Take the time to figure it out, and then learn with purpose to make that vision a reality.

Learning with Intentionality

Learning with purpose is about pursuing knowledge that resonates with your core values and life goals. It's more than just gathering information; it's about intentional growth and development that aligns with who you want to be. Let's assess how well you're embracing purposeful learning in your life.

Ask yourself the following questions and rate yourself from 0 to 5, with 0 being "Never," 1 "Rarely," 2 "Sometimes," 3 "Often," 4 "Usually," and 5 "Always":

_____ I seek to acquire learning that is consistent with my values.

_____ I feel that my life has a positive purpose.

_____ I am concerned about humanitarian issues and seek to understand them.

____ I have a set of values that consistently guide my decisions in life.

____ I engage regularly in character-building activities.

____ **TOTAL**

Now, take all your numbers and add them up to get your total score. For example, if you rated yourself a four in every area, your total score would be 20. Here's how to interpret your results:

- 21 - 25: Excellent! You are highly intentional about your learning and growth, ensuring it aligns with your values and purpose. Continue nurturing this path to enhance your personal and professional development.

- 16 - 20: Good job, but there's room for deeper alignment. Focus on areas where you scored lower to strengthen your commitment to purposeful learning.

- 15 or below: Don't worry. You can always start aligning your learning with your values and goals. Consider taking small steps to cultivate purposeful growth.

Learning with purpose is about more than just knowledge acquisition; it's about growing in a direction that enriches your life and aligns with your values. Here are three steps to help you enhance purposeful learning:

Set Clear Learning Goals: Identify specific areas of knowledge or skills you want to develop. Write down your learning objectives and break them into manageable steps. Whether through reading, online courses, or workshops, have a clear plan for achieving your goals.

Align Learning with Values: Reflect on your core values and ensure that the topics you choose to learn about resonate with those values. This alignment will keep you motivated and ensure your learning contributes meaningfully to your growth and purpose.

Engage in Character-Building Activities: Look for opportunities to engage in activities that build character and enhance your understanding of the world. This could include volunteering, mentoring others, or participating in community service. These experiences provide valuable life lessons and help you grow holistically.

By focusing on these steps, you'll find yourself growing in ways that are enriching and deeply aligned with your personal and professional goals.

Go FurtherFaster in Your Spiritual Wellbeing

Spiritual Wellbeing is about nurturing a deep connection with your inner self and aligning your life with your core values and beliefs. It's about understanding what drives you, finding purpose, and living in harmony with your spiritual principles. This section explored two vital principles for enhancing Spiritual Wellbeing: Listen To Truth and Learn With Purpose.

Listen To Truth: This principle is a call to seek and embrace truth in every aspect of your life. Embracing truth is about more than just honesty; it's about aligning your actions and decisions with your deepest values and beliefs. By listening to truth, you cultivate a life of integrity and authenticity. This alignment cultivates a sense of inner peace and clarity, allowing you to make choices that resonate with your true self. Embracing this principle helps you remain grounded, especially in times of uncertainty, and provides a strong moral compass to guide your decisions and actions.

Learn With Purpose: This principle focuses on intentionally pursuing knowledge that aligns with your values and life goals. It encourages you to seek out learning opportunities that contribute to your growth and enhance your understanding of yourself and the world around you. By learning with purpose, you gain knowledge and enrich your spirit, fostering a sense of direction and meaning in your life. Being purposeful reminds you to engage in lifelong learning as a tool for self-improvement and personal development, ensuring that your journey is aligned with your spiritual aspirations.

Embracing both principles helps cultivate a spiritual life rich with meaning, integrity, and growth. This approach allows you to navigate your life with clarity and purpose, ensuring that each step you take is in harmony with who you truly are. Through this alignment and intentional learning, you can go FurtherFaster in your spiritual journey, discovering deeper connections to yourself and the greater world around you.

Section 10
Vocational Wellbeing

Vocational Wellbeing is the ability to actively pursue career ambitions while deriving personal fulfillment from one's profession. It involves feeling content with the current state of your job and the future direction of your career and skill development.

If you are satisfied with your career, it's important to take proactive steps to maintain and enhance that satisfaction. Without continuous growth, even a fulfilling job can stagnate over time, leading to a loss of motivation and engagement. By nurturing your professional life with intention, you ensure that your career remains a source of personal and professional fulfillment.

If you're not currently in a good place with your Vocational Wellbeing, don't wait—take action now. Ignoring this critical area of your life can lead to burnout, dissatisfaction, and a lack of purpose. The longer you allow discontentment to fester, the more likely it will impact other areas of your wellbeing, such as your mental and emotional health. Given how much time we spend working, it's vital that your vocation is not only productive but fulfilling. A career that drains you will eventually diminish your overall quality of life, making it harder to achieve happiness.

Whether you're thriving or striving in your career right now, consider these FurtherFaster Principles to enhance your Vocational Wellbeing.

To Go Further: Become an Expert

Developing deep expertise in your field is essential for long-term career success and fulfillment. Mastery in a specific area ensures job security, recognition, and advancement opportunities, positioning you as a valuable resource and potential leader. Without this deep expertise, you may struggle to establish credibility and stand out. Investing in expertise builds a stable foundation for sustained professional growth.

To Go Faster: Do Many Things

Alternatively, gaining diverse experiences and skills quickly enhances your professional effectiveness. Doing many things makes you versatile and adaptable, equipping you to tackle various challenges and seize new opportunities. Without a broad range of experiences, you risk limiting your growth and becoming less relevant in a dynamic job market. Diversifying your skill set ensures you remain competitive and prepared for evolving roles.

Vocational Wellbeing requires you to invest in both deepening your expertise and broadening your experiences.

Think of it like a football game: Going deep is like a long pass to the end zone, aiming for longevity and mastery in your career—you're headed for the touchdown. Meanwhile, going wide is like gaining short, consistent yardage with quick wins and immediate improvements. Each short pass or rush adds up over time, helping you move forward, adapt, and respond to changing opportunities on the field. Embrace both strategies to cultivate a fulfilling and resilient career, helping you go FurtherFaster in your vocational journey.

Further Principle

Become an Expert

"Researchers have settled on what they believe is the magic number for true expertise: ten thousand hours."

- Malcolm Gladwell

Becoming an expert involves more than just accumulating knowledge; it requires a long-term commitment to mastering a particular field or skill through dedicated practice, continuous learning, and relentless pursuit of excellence. This principle is about immersing oneself deeply in a chosen area to build substantial expertise and become a valuable resource within the industry or community.

A person who embodies this principle invests significant time and effort into honing their craft, recognizing that expertise is not achieved overnight but through years of focused practice and intentional growth. They engage in consistent study, seek out mentorship, and actively pursue opportunities that challenge their understanding and skills. This dedication to mastery provides a solid foundation for career success, financial stability, and personal fulfillment.

The importance of becoming an expert cannot be overstated. Research has shown that individuals with specialized expertise in their field tend to earn more than their non-expert counterparts, with some studies indicating a 20% higher earning potential for recognized experts [57]. This financial benefit reflects the value that expertise brings to the table—employers and clients are willing to pay a premium for the insights and skills that only an expert can provide.

Moreover, research in decision-making psychology also shows that experts are often able to make decisions faster and more accurately than non-experts. For example, Kahneman and Klein found that experts' ability to recognize patterns and make rapid decisions is often double that of non-experts [58]. This enhanced decision-making ability is particularly valuable in high-stakes or time-sensitive situations, where expertise can make the difference between success and failure.

Becoming an expert is about developing depth in a chosen field, which enhances skills, builds confidence, and encourages continuous personal and professional growth. In a world that increasingly values specialization, expertise is not just an asset—it is a necessity for those who wish to stand out, lead, and thrive.

Mastering the Craft of Expertise

My journey into expertise began with a rigorous academic path. I was the first student at my university to enter a combined Bachelor-Master accelerated degree plan, completing my Master of Science in Computer Science in the time it typically took others to finish their Bachelor's degree. This intense academic endeavor laid a solid foundation for my deep expertise in technology—a field I have always been passionate about.

While I went on to earn an MBA and later a PhD in Emotional Intelligence, my tech background has remained a constant in my professional life.

However, my journey to expertise wasn't just shaped by formal education. A significant part of my growth came from personal experiences—experimenting with new technologies on my own, teaching others, and learning from real-world challenges.

Mentorship played a critical role as well; I've had the privilege of working alongside brilliant minds and learning from their successes and failures. Asking questions, seeking feedback from peers and experts, and reading voraciously about industry trends have all contributed to my understanding.

Becoming an expert is about more than just degrees or job titles. It's a relentless commitment to continuous learning, curiosity, and a willingness to dive deep into your field. For me, expertise has come not just from classrooms or textbooks but from hands-on experiences, conversations with other professionals, and even the trial-and-error of figuring things out on my own.

This principle applies universally, whether you're pursuing a relational career, side hustle, or financial mastery. The world is full of noise, but it craves authentic voices—those with genuine knowledge and insight gained through dedication, practice, and real-world engagement. You could be that expert—the one who stands out not just because of credentials but because of the depth of your understanding and your ability to contribute meaningfully to your field.

Becoming an Expert

Becoming an expert in your field is about honing your skills, dedicating yourself to continuous improvement, and mastering your craft with a passion. Expertise comes from a commitment to excellence and an ongoing quest to learn and grow. Let's evaluate how well you are progressing toward becoming an expert in your chosen field.

Ask yourself the following questions and rate yourself from 0 to 5, with 0 being "Never," 1 "Rarely," 2 "Sometimes," 3 "Often," 4 "Usually," and 5 "Always":

____ I engage regularly in activities related to my work, avocation, or job.

____ I have a 'vocation' that aligns well with my core values.

____ I manage stress effectively and maintain a healthy approach to my vocation.

Vocational Wellbeing | 175

_____ I look forward to performing the activities involved in my 'vocation.'

_____ I consistently deepen my knowledge and experiences in my expertise.

_____ **TOTAL**

Now, take all your numbers and add them up to get your total score. For example, if you rated yourself a four in every area, your total score would be 20. Here's how to interpret your results:

- 21 - 25: Outstanding! You are well on your way to becoming an expert in your field. Keep up the commitment to learning and refining your craft to achieve even greater mastery.

- 16 - 20: Good progress, but there's room for growth. Focus on areas where you scored lower to deepen your expertise and refine your skills.

- 15 or below: It's time to focus on developing your expertise. Start by setting specific learning goals and seeking opportunities to enhance your skills.

Becoming an expert requires dedication, passion, and a willingness to learn continuously. Here are three steps to help you accelerate your journey toward mastery:

Commit to Continuous Learning: Dedicate a specific time each week to learning about your field's latest trends, techniques, and developments. This could involve reading industry journals, attending workshops, enrolling in advanced courses, listening to podcasts, following experts on social media, going to conferences, or lunch and learns. Staying updated with the latest information will ensure you remain at the forefront of your field.

Practice Deliberately: Apply your knowledge in real-world situations and seek out challenges that stretch your abilities. Regularly practice your skills and ask for feedback from mentors or colleagues to identify areas for improvement. Remember, mastery is achieved through repetition and refinement over time.

Teach and Share Your Expertise: Look for opportunities to share your knowledge with others, whether through writing articles, giving presentations, or mentoring junior colleagues. Teaching is a powerful way to reinforce your learning, deepen your understanding, and position yourself as a thought leader in your field.

By embracing these steps, you'll cultivate the skills and knowledge necessary to become a recognized expert in your area, opening doors to new opportunities and achievements.

Faster Principle

Do Many Things

"There's value in creating and living a 'total life' with diverse interests, activities, relationships, and pursuits; it's called 'living in more than one world.'"

- Bruce Rosenstein

Doing many things emphasizes the importance of exploring diverse interests and engaging in a variety of activities. This approach allows individuals to enrich their experiences and broaden their horizons, leading to a more dynamic and fulfilling life.

A person who embodies this principle is inherently curious and adventurous, constantly seeking new opportunities and embracing different experiences. They discover new passions and talents by venturing into new areas and doing different things, nurturing personal growth and adaptability. Engaging in various pursuits prevents monotony, encourages creativity, and builds resilience, all contributing to a multifaceted and fulfilling life.

Research supports the value of doing many things. A study by the University of Pennsylvania found that individuals with diverse career experiences were 24% more likely to be promoted to leadership positions compared to those with more linear career paths [59]. This finding suggests that varied experiences can significantly enhance career advancement by equipping individuals with a broader skill set and perspective.

Implementing the Do Many Things principle doesn't mean abandoning your current career path. In fact, exploring diverse interests outside of work can complement your primary vocation and offer immediate benefits. For example, learning a new language could open doors to international opportunities, or starting a side project like photography might nurture creativity that enhances problem-solving in your day-to-day job. Volunteering in a different field can also help develop leadership skills, while hobbies like painting or writing can reduce stress and provide a refreshing mental reset.

Engaging in multiple activities and hobbies also boosts creativity and innovation in the workplace. Exposure to different domains can spark new connections and ideas, thereby enhancing overall productivity and job satisfaction. A study by Amabile showed that engaging in diverse interests can enhance creative problem-solving abilities and innovation [60].

These studies and insights demonstrate the value of doing many things. By diversifying one's experiences and skills, individuals can achieve greater career growth, enhance creativity, and find overall life satisfaction. Whether it's taking up a new hobby, volunteering in your community, or pursuing a side hustle, embracing this principle leads to a vibrant, meaningful life filled with growth, discovery, and resilience.

A Personal Plea: Do Many Things

I recall a pivotal moment during my time as a leading innovation executive at a healthcare institution. We were making incredible strides—pioneering 3D printing for bone replacements, developing mobile apps for home care, and advancing robotic brain surgeries. Yet, amid these technological achievements, a doctor in our system took his own life. That tragic event hit me hard. What good were these innovations if we couldn't ensure the wellbeing of our own people? This led me to study burnout in helping professions and eventually pursue a PhD in Emotional Intelligence.

I went from being a heads-down coder with little emotional insight to someone who now studies and teaches it for a living. Branching out of my initial technology career and exploring new fields led me to discover a deep passion for people, start several companies, and ultimately write this book. If I had stuck solely to my original skill set, I would have missed out on all these opportunities for growth and fulfillment.

Each wellbeing aspect I've discussed in this book stems from both deep research and real-life application. I would not have been able to write this book if I hadn't taken my own advice and pursued a variety of interests. I've dived into emotional intelligence, environmental positioning, financial planning, intellectual studies, organizational strategies, physical fitness, recreational activities, relational wins and losses, spiritual practices, and vocational leaps. In exploring each of these areas, I've learned what works, what doesn't, what's productive, and what can truly benefit you.

Embracing New Experiences for Growth

Doing many things is about stepping out of your comfort zone, exploring diverse activities, and gaining valuable insights from each experience. It's about continuously learning and growing by embracing a variety of interests and challenges. Let's assess how well you are embracing new experiences in your life.

Ask yourself the following questions and rate yourself from 0 to 5, with 0 being "Never," 1 "Rarely," 2 "Sometimes," 3 "Often," 4 "Usually," and 5 "Always":

____ I regularly pursue new skills or certifications to stay competitive and relevant in my field.

____ I manage my time intentionally to incorporate both vocational activities and leisure.

_____ I feel there are enough challenges and variety in my life.

_____ I gain valuable experiences through the diverse activities I engage in.

_____ I apply lessons learned from career setbacks to enable future success.

_____ **TOTAL**

Now, take all your numbers and add them up to get your total score. For example, if you rated yourself a four in every area, your total score would be 20. Here's how to interpret your results:

- 21 - 25: Excellent! You actively embrace new experiences and challenges, contributing to a rich and varied life. Keep exploring and learning.

- 16 - 20: Good job, but there's room for growth. Focus on areas where you scored lower to expand your experiences and enhance personal growth.

- 15 or below: It's time to step out of your comfort zone and do something new. Start by setting small, achievable goals to broaden your horizons.

Exploring diverse experiences isn't just about variety; it's about learning, growing, and finding fulfillment. Here are three steps to help you do many things:

Find Something New to Explore: Identify an activity, hobby, or skill you've always been curious about. Whether it's learning to play a musical instrument, taking up a new sport, or starting a creative project—take the plunge. Embrace the excitement of doing something new.

Embrace and Learn from Failure: Understand that failure is an essential part of the learning process. When stepping into new experiences, don't fear failure; instead, view it as a valuable opportunity to learn and grow. Reflect on what went wrong, what you can improve, and how to apply these lessons in the future.

Reflect and Apply Insights: After engaging in a new experience, take some time to reflect on what you've learned and how it has impacted you. Consider how these insights can be applied to other areas of your life or inspire you to do even more new activities. This reflection will help solidify the learning and encourage continuous exploration.

By actively embracing new experiences and learning from them, you'll enrich your life with diversity, growth, and endless possibilities for personal development.

Go FurtherFaster in Your Vocational Wellbeing

Vocational Wellbeing is about aligning your career with your core values and finding joy and purpose in your work. It's not just about what you do but how and why you do it. This section explored two foundational principles to enhance Vocational Wellbeing: Become An Expert and Do Many Things.

Become An Expert: This principle encourages you to fully commit to mastering your chosen field. It's about dedicating yourself to continuous learning, refining your skills, and striving for excellence in your profession. Mastery is not achieved overnight; it requires persistence, curiosity, and a willingness to fervently pursue your craft. Becoming an expert is about becoming a valuable resource in your industry, gaining the respect and trust of your peers, and experiencing a deep sense of fulfillment from your achievements. Embracing this principle transforms your work from a job into a vocation, a true calling where you find both personal and professional satisfaction.

Do Many Things: This principle advocates for embracing a wide range of experiences beyond your primary career focus. Broadening your interests encourages you to step out of your comfort zone and explore new fields, hobbies, and interests. Doing so broadens your perspective, acquires new skills, and develops a more adaptable mindset. This diversity enriches your personal life and enhances your professional capacity, allowing you to approach your primary vocation with fresh insights and innovative thinking. Exploring multiple avenues also prepares you to navigate an ever-changing job market, equipping you with the versatility needed to pivot when necessary.

By incorporating both principles, you craft a career path that is both successful and deeply fulfilling. You become a master of your domain while remaining open to new opportunities and learning. This dual approach enables you to go FurtherFaster in your vocational journey, achieving a career that is rewarding, meaningful, and aligned with your true self. Embrace both mastery and exploration to unlock the full potential of your professional life.

Next Steps
Your Journey Begins Here

Congratulations!

If you've made it this far, you're already ahead of the curve. Most people never finish the books they start, so the fact that you've made it to the end tells me a lot about you. You're serious about making a change. You're ready to take action, and I want you to know—I'm proud of you. This is no small feat.

But here's the truth: **This isn't the end—it's just the beginning.** Moving forward, what matters now is how you use what you've learned.

Throughout the book, you've explored the Further and Faster principles in each area of wellbeing:

- **Further** principles focus on longevity, sustainability, and personal wellbeing—the "slow and steady" progress that builds a solid foundation for life.

- **Faster** principles emphasize quick wins, professional success, and measurable achievements—helping you make progress today.

These principles and all areas of wellbeing we've explored throughout the book—emotional, financial, physical, and beyond—are all interconnected. You don't need to tackle everything at once. Small steps in one area can pull the others along with it, leading to unexpected gains in other areas.

For example, starting a fitness routine might not only improve your physical health but might also boost your confidence to rekindle a relationship, help you save money by dining out less, or give you the energy to start a new hobby.

So, don't just read this book once and leave it on a shelf to collect dust. Keep it close. Use it as a resource whenever you feel stuck or need a boost in any area of your life. This book and these principles are meant to help you over and over and over to reach whatever new goals appear on the path in front of you.

How to Get the Most From Your Further-Faster Experience

This book is designed to help you identify where you are today and where you want to focus next. Take a moment to reflect:

- Which area of wellbeing spoke to you the most?
- Where do you feel the biggest opportunity for growth lies?

As I've already said, you don't have to address everything at once. Pick one area that feels the most important right now, revisit that chapter, and start working through the strategies and activities.

If you'd like a little extra clarity or guidance, I encourage you to take our FREE online assessment to see where you stand across all areas of wellbeing. The assessment will give you a consolidated report and personalized recommendations to help you take action confidently. You can find the details for the free assessment on page 189.

If you feel like you could use personal guidance, I also recommend connecting with a FurtherFaster coach. Our certified coaches can walk you through your results and help you build a strategy tailored to your goals—whether you need help with long-term planning or are looking to hit the ground running.

And if you enjoyed this book and think someone else in your life could benefit from it, buy them a copy as a gift. Gifting someone the ability to see life differently and make different choices is something that can't be understated.

Thank You!

Thank you for trusting me with your time, energy, and focus. I hope this book has given you the clarity, tools, and inspiration you need to move forward. **I'd love to hear how this book has helped you**—feel free to send your success stories, questions, or feedback to my email or through the website. Your journey matters, and I'm honored to be a part of it.

Jeff
jeff.frey@furtherfaster.com

Take Your Life to the Next Level with the FREE FurtherFaster Assessment!

Inside every chapter, you've had the opportunity to self-assess and reflect. But what if you could quickly and easily answer the same questions and get a completely customized report with recommendations just for you?

Would you like that? Would that be worth its weight in gold? If so, let me introduce you to…

The FurtherFaster Assessment (FREE for Readers of this Book!)

In less than 10 minutes, you'll not only receive a deeper insight into the ten areas we discussed in this book, but you'll also get a custom plan tailored to your unique scores so you can…

- Create quick wins and build momentum in your life
- Boost your progress toward your goals
- Achieve sustainable, long-term growth
- And much, much more!

How It Works

- Visit www.FurtherFaster.com/bookoffer.

- Enter this exclusive promo code to unlock the full assessment: **FURTHERFASTER2025**.

- Answer the questions to instantly get your custom report and recommendations.

There's no better time to act than right now! Take the free assessment, unlock the insights you need, and start moving FurtherFaster!

About the Author

Jeff Frey, PhD, is the author of *FurtherFaster* and the founder of a company dedicated to helping business owners and change-makers discover longevity and accelerate success in entrepreneurship, leadership, and overall wellbeing. Drawing from academic research and real-world experience, Jeff's FurtherFaster framework blends strategic insight with practical methods to empower professionals and organizations to achieve faster, more sustainable growth. His approach focuses on cultivating purpose-driven leadership, ensuring personal wellbeing, and preventing burnout.

Throughout his career, Jeff has held leadership roles across healthcare, technology, and education. He has been a key figure in creating academic and healthcare innovation centers, transforming pioneering research into successful businesses. He has founded several companies and created programs that equip professionals with the skills they need to thrive in today's job market. Jeff has also developed degree programs and taught at prestigious institutions, earning recognition such as MBA Professor of the Year. These experiences have directly shaped the FurtherFaster Principles, integrating his work in emotional intelligence, leadership, and innovation to provide actionable tools for leaders to succeed without sacrificing personal wellbeing. His message has led to being featured in well-known magazines, keynote invitations at conferences, and numerous recorded webinars and interviews.

Outside of his professional life, Jeff is a devoted husband and father of two boys. He is passionate about music, triathlon sports, and mentoring young entrepreneurs, always seeking to lead by example. These personal interests reflect the core of the FurtherFaster philosophy—encouraging others to achieve their goals without compromising their health, happiness, or relationships. Jeff's dedication to living a FurtherFaster life aligns with the principles he shares, empowering others to build resilience and find fulfillment in both professional work and personal life.

Looking for a Dynamic Speaker to Elevate Your Next Event?

Looking for an engaging and insightful speaker who can inspire your audience to accelerate their success while maintaining wellbeing? Need a presenter who combines real-world experience with actionable strategies in emotional intelligence, wellbeing, leadership, or personal development? If so, Jeff Frey, PhD is the speaker you've been looking for!

Why Choose Jeff Frey, PhD for Your Event?

- **Expert in Accelerating Success:** As the author of *FurtherFaster* and the creator of the FurtherFaster Principles, Jeff empowers individuals and organizations to achieve their goals more quickly and sustainably by blending practical insights with innovative strategies.

- **Real-World Experience:** With over 30 years of experience spanning technology, healthcare, education, and entrepreneurship, Jeff draws on his diverse background as a C-level executive, founder of successful companies, and an academic leader.

- **Award-Winning Educator:** Teaching at top institutions like Rice University and The Citadel, where he was named MBA Professor of the Year for two consecutive years, Jeff's approach integrates practical wisdom with cutting-edge research.

- **Engaging Storyteller:** Known for his high energy and relatable storytelling, Jeff connects with audiences from various backgrounds, leaving them inspired and equipped with tools to implement immediately.

- **Customized Presentations:** Each of Jeff's talks is tailored to the specific needs of your audience, ensuring relevance and maximum impact.

Presentation Topics Include:

- **The 5 Keys to Accelerate Success with the FurtherFaster Principles**
  Perfect for professionals seeking to fast-track their personal and career growth.

- **From Burnout to Breakthrough: Harnessing Emotional Intelligence for Sustainable Leadership**
  Ideal for leaders aiming to enhance resilience and prevent burnout.

- **Combining AI and EI: Elevating Leadership in the Digital Age**
  Great for organizations looking to integrate technology with human-centric leadership.

- **Entrepreneurship Unleashed: Turning Innovative Ideas into Successful Ventures**
  Perfect for aspiring entrepreneurs and startup founders.

- **Building Purpose-Driven Teams: Strategies for Cultivating a Thriving Organizational Culture**
  Designed for managers and HR professionals focused on team development.

What Event Planners and Attendees Say About Jeff Frey, PhD:

"We wish every speaker was a Jeff. His dedication and adaptability set him apart. Whether working with small teams or larger audiences, his attention to detail, practical insights, and commitment to excellence shine. Dr. Frey has a remarkable ability to bridge technical expertise with human connection, delivering engaging sessions that inspire action and foster collaboration. We are excited about future opportunities to bring Jeff back!"

— Teresa C., PMO and QA Manager, Founderz, Spain

"The practical strategies in the series of hands-on workshops Dr. Frey has conducted have made a significant impact on our team's performance. His emotional and artificial intelligence talks were exactly what we needed to get to the next level."

— Douglas F., VP Business, SWORD@BP, Houston, Texas, US

"An amazing experience! Jeff Frey brought his knowledge, work experience, and passion to educate us and provide valuable insights on important topics around talent strategies, performance, and organizational culture. So informative and super engaging."
— Angie N., HR Talent Manager, SHRM Talent Conference, Las Vegas, Nevada, US

Book Jeff Frey, PhD for Your Next Event

Don't miss the opportunity to bring Jeff Frey's expertise and passion to your audience. Whether it's a keynote presentation, workshop, or seminar, he will deliver a memorable experience that inspires action.

Contact Information:
Email: jeff.frey@furtherfaster.com
Phone: (832) 384-5167
Website: furtherfaster.com

Motivate and Inspire Others!

Retail $24.95

Special Quantity Discounts

5-20 Books	$21.95
21-99 Books	$19.95
100-499 Books	$17.95
500-999 Books	$15.95
1,000+ Books	$13.95

Special Discount Pricing is subject to change.
Please contact us for final pricing options.

To Place an Order Contact:
www.FurtherFaster.com
jeff.frey@furtherfaster.com
(832) 384-5167

Works Cited

[1] Fredrickson, Barbara L. "The Role of Positive Emotions in Positive Psychology: The Broaden-and-Build Theory of Positive Emotions." *American Psychologist*, vol. 56, no. 3, 2001, pp. 218–26.

[2] Van Bommel, T. "The Power of Empathy in Times of Crisis and Beyond." *Catalyst*, 2021.

[3] Powell, P. A. "Individual Differences in Emotion Regulation Moderate the Associations between Empathy and Affective Distress." *Motivation and Emotion*, vol. 42, 2018, pp. 602–13, doi:10.1007/s11031-018-9684-4.

[4] Slemp, G. R., et al. "Interpersonal Supports for Basic Psychological Needs and Their Relations with Motivation, Wellbeing, and Performance: A Meta-Analysis." *Journal of Personality and Social Psychology*, advance online publication, 2024, doi:10.1037/pspi0000459.

[5] Di Domenico, S. I., and Ryan, R. M. "The Emerging Neuroscience of Intrinsic Motivation: A New Frontier in Self-Determination Research." *Frontiers in Human Neuroscience*, vol. 11, 2017, p. 145, doi:10.3389/fnhum.2017.00145.

[6] Reisinger, H., and D. Fetterer. "Forget Flexibility. Your Employees Want Autonomy." *Harvard Business Review*, 2021, p. 29.

[7] Batson, C. D. "These Things Called Empathy: Eight Related but Distinct Phenomena." *The Social Neuroscience of Empathy*, 2009, pp. 3–16.

[8] Evans, G. W., and J. M. McCoy. "When Buildings Don't Work: The Role of Architecture in Human Health." *Journal of Environmental Psychology*, vol. 18, no. 1, 1998, pp. 85–94.

[9] Yeung, J. W. K., Zhang, Z., and T. Y. Kim. "Volunteering and Health Benefits in General Adults: Cumulative Effects and Forms." *BMC Public Health*, vol. 18, no. 1, 2017, p. 8, doi:10.1186/s12889-017-4561-8.

[10] Spera, C., Ghertner, R., Nerino, A., and A. DiTommaso. "Volunteering as a Pathway to Employment: Does Volunteering Increase Odds of Finding a Job for the Out of Work?" *Corporation for National and Community Service, Office of Research and Evaluation*, Washington, DC, 2013.

[11] Boyatzis, Richard E., Melvin L. Smith, and Nancy Blaize. "Developing Sustainable Leaders through Coaching and Compassion." *Academy of Management Learning and Education*, vol. 5, 2006, pp. 8–24, doi:10.5465/amle.2006.20388381.

[12] Saxbe, D. E., and R. L. Repetti. "No Place Like Home: Home Tours Correlate with Daily Patterns of Mood and Cortisol." *Personality and Social Psychology Bulletin*, vol. 36, no. 1, 2010, pp. 71–81.

[13] Gallup. "Employee Burnout: Causes and Cures." *Gallup*, 2020, www.gallup.com/workplace/282659/employee-burnout-perspective-paper.aspx.

[14] Knight, Phil. *Shoe Dog: A Memoir by the Creator of Nike*. Scribner, 2016.

[15] Batdorf, E. "Key Savings Statistics and Trends in 2024." *Forbes Advisor*, 29 June 2023, www.forbes.com/advisor/banking/savings/american-savings-statistics/.

[16] U.S. Bureau of Economic Analysis. "Personal Saving Rate [PSAVERT]." *Federal Reserve Bank of St. Louis*, 29 Aug. 2024, fred.stlouisfed.org/series/PSAVERT.

[17] Councilor, Buchanan, and Mitchell. "Building an Emergency Fund: Your Financial Safety Net." *Councilor, Buchanan, and Mitchell*, 18 July 2024, www.cbmcpa.com/2024/07/18/building-emergency-fund-financial-safety-net.

[18] Medina, J. C. "8 Ways to Use Financial Mindfulness to Enhance Your Life." *Forbes*, 7 May 2024, www.forbes.com/sites/financialfinesse/2024/05/07/financial-mindfulness-the-key-to-enhancing-your-financial-life/.

[19] Kumar, Amit, Matthew Killingsworth, and Thomas Gilovich. "Spending on Doing Promotes More Moment-to-Moment Happiness than Spending on Having." *Journal of Experimental Social Psychology*, vol. 88, 2020, doi:10.1016/j.jesp.2020.103971.

[20] Fleming, J. "Consumers Spending More, Just Not on Things They Want." *Gallup*, 11 July 2014.

[21] Quicken. "10 Budget Categories That Belong in Your Plan." *Quicken*, 23 Feb. 2024, www.quicken.com/blog/budget-categories/.

[22] National Institute on Aging. "Cognitive Health and Older Adults." *U.S. Department of Health and Human Services*, www.nia.nih.gov/health/brain-health/cognitive-health-and-older-adults.

[23] Goodnow, Jacqueline J. "Children's Household Work: Its Nature and Functions." *Psychological Bulletin*, vol. 103, no. 1, 1988, pp. 5–26, doi:10.1037/0033-2909.103.1.5.

[24] Tepper, D. L., T. J. Howell, and P. C. Bennett. "Executive Functions and Household Chores: Does Engagement in Chores Predict Children's Cognition?" *Australian Occupational Therapy Journal*, vol. 69, no. 5, 2022, pp. 585–98, doi:10.1111/1440-1630.12822.

[25] Bradberry, Travis, and Jean Greaves. *Emotional Intelligence 2.0.* TalentSmart, 2009.

[26] Pisano, Gary P. "You Need an Innovation Strategy." *Harvard Business Review*, vol. 93, no. 6, 2015, pp. 44–54.

[27] McKinsey & Company. "How COVID-19 Has Pushed Companies over the Technology Tipping Point—and Transformed Business Forever." *McKinsey & Company*, 2021, www.mckinsey.com/capabilities/strategy-and-corporate-finance/our-insights/how-covid-19-has-pushed-companies-over-the-technology-tipping-point-and-transformed-business-forever.

[28] Banholzer, M., L. LaBerge, A. West, and E. Williams. "How Innovative Companies Leverage Tech to Outperform." *McKinsey & Company*, 14 Dec. 2023, www.mckinsey.com/capabilities/strategy-and-corporate-finance/our-insights/how-innovative-companies-leverage-tech-to-outperform.

[29] University of Phoenix. "Career Optimism Index: A Study on American Workers and Career Resilience." *University of Phoenix Career Institute*, 2021.

[30] Jagannath, S., Birgitta Gatersleben, and Eleanor Ratcliffe. "Flexibility of the Home and Residents' Psychological Wellbeing." *Journal of Environmental Psychology*, 2024, doi:10.1016/j.jenvp.2024.102333.

[31] Murphy, A. "Americans Spend an Average of 2.5 Days Each Year Looking for Lost Items." *New York Post*, 23 May 2017, nypost.com/2017/05/23/americans-spend-an-average-of-2-5-days-each-year-looking-for-lost-items/.

[32] McKinsey & Company. "The Social Economy: Unlocking Value and Productivity through Social Technologies." *McKinsey Global Institute*, 2012, www.mckinsey.com/industries/technology-media-and-telecommunications/our-insights/the-social-economy.

[33] Doodle. *The State of Meetings Report.* 2019, en.blog.doodle.com/the-true-cost-of-bad-meetings/.

[34] World Health Organization. "Physical Activity." *World Health Organization*, 2020, www.who.int/news-room/fact-sheets/detail/physical-activity.

[35] Harvard Health Publishing. "The Benefits of Exercise: How to Get Started." *Harvard Medical School*, 2021, www.health.harvard.edu/staying-healthy/the-importance-of-exercise-and-the-many-ways-to-get-moving.

[36] National Sleep Foundation. "How Much Sleep Do We Really Need?" *National Sleep Foundation*, 2020, www.sleepfoundation.org/how-sleep-works/how-much-sleep-do-we-really-need.

[37] Roenigk, A. "How LeBron James, Tom Brady, and Other Athletes Get the Best Sleep." *ESPN*, 20 Dec. 2017, www.espn.com/nba/story/_/id/21795766/how-lebron-james-tom-brady-athletes-get-best-sleep.

[38] Slack. "The Surprising Connection between After-Hours Work and Decreased Productivity." *Slack*, 5 Dec. 2023, slack.com/blog/news/the-surprising-connection-between-after-hours-work-and-decreased-productivity.

[39] Guthold, Regina, et al. "Worldwide Trends in Insufficient Physical Activity from 2001 to 2016: A Pooled Analysis of 358 Population-Based Surveys with 1.9 Million Participants." *The Lancet Global Health*, vol. 6, no. 10, 2018, pp. 1077–86, doi:10.1016/S2214-109X(18)30357-7.

[40] U.S. Department of Health and Human Services. *Physical Activity Guidelines for Americans.* 2nd ed., 2018, health.gov/sites/default/files/2019-09/Physical_Activity_Guidelines_2nd_edition.pdf.

[41] Diaz, K. M., et al. "Potential Effects on Mortality of Replacing Sedentary Time with Short Sedentary Bouts or Physical Activity: A National Cohort Study." *American Journal of Epidemiology*, vol. 188, no. 3, 2019, pp. 537–44, doi:10.1093/aje/kwy271.

[42] Pressman, S. D., et al. "Association of Enjoyable Leisure Activities with Psychological and Physical Well-Being." *Psychosomatic Medicine*, vol. 71, no. 7, 2009, pp. 725–32, doi:10.1097/PSY.0b013e3181ad7978.

[43] Locke, E. A., K. N. Shaw, L. M. Saari, and G. P. Latham. "Goal Setting and Task Performance: 1969–1980." *Psychological Bulletin*, vol. 90, no. 1, 1981, pp. 125–52, doi:10.1037/0033-2909.90.1.125.

[44] Martín-Talavera, L., Ó. Gavín-Chocano, G. Sanz-Junoy, and D. Molero. "Self-Concept and Self-Esteem, Determinants of Greater Life Satisfaction in Mountain and Climbing Technicians and Athletes." *European Journal of Investigation in Health, Psychology and Education*, vol. 13, no. 7, 2023, pp. 1188–1201, doi:10.3390/ejihpe13070088.

[45] Clear, James. *Atomic Habits: An Easy & Proven Way to Build Good Habits and Break Bad Ones*. Penguin Books, 2018.

[46] Lewis, David. *Galaxy Stress Research*. Mindlab International, Sussex University, 2009.

[47] Holt-Lunstad, Julianne, Timothy B. Smith, and J. Bradley Layton. "Social Relationships and Mortality Risk: A Meta-Analytic Review." *PLOS Medicine*, vol. 7, no. 7, 2010, doi:10.1371/journal.pmed.1000316.

[48] "2nd Generation Study." *Harvard Medical School*, 2015, www.adultdevelopmentstudy.org/.

[49] Cox, Daniel A. "The State of American Friendship: Change, Challenges, and Loss." *American Perspectives Survey*, 8 June 2021, www.americansurveycenter.org/research/the-state-of-american-friendship-change-challenges-and-loss/.

[50] Holt-Lunstad, Julianne, Timothy B. Smith, and J. Bradley Layton. "Social Relationships and Mortality Risk: A Meta-Analytic Review." *PLOS Medicine*, vol. 7, no. 7, 2010, doi:10.1371/journal.pmed.1000316.

[51] Kringelbach, M. L., and K. C. Berridge. "The Neuroscience of Happiness and Pleasure." *Social Research*, vol. 77, no. 2, 2010, pp. 659–78.

[52] Miller, Lisa. *The Awakened Brain: The New Science of Spirituality and Our Quest for an Inspired Life*. Random House, 2021.

[53] Shiba, K., et al. "Purpose in Life and 8-Year Mortality by Gender and Race/Ethnicity among Older Adults in the U.S." *Preventive Medicine*, 2022, p. 164, doi:10.1016/j.ypmed.2022.107310.

[54] Simons, Tony. *The Integrity Dividend: Leading by the Power of Your Word*. John Wiley & Sons, 2008.

[55] Ray, Brian D. *Research Facts on Homeschooling*. National Home Education Research Institute, 2017, www.nheri.org/research-facts-on-homeschooling/.

[56] Boyle, Patricia A., et al. "Purpose in Life Is Associated with Mortality among Community-Dwelling Older Persons." *Psychosomatic Medicine*, vol. 72, no. 6, 2010, pp. 535–39, doi:10.1097/PSY.0b013e3181e9b493.

[57] Gjerde, K. A., and W. D. Albrecht. "The Impacts of Research and Teaching on Student Evaluation of Faculty Performance." *Journal of Accounting Education*, vol. 17, nos. 2–3, 1998, pp. 289–301, doi:10.1016/S0748-5751(99)00021-7.

[58] Kahneman, Daniel, and Gary Klein. "Conditions for Intuitive Expertise: A Failure to Disagree." *American Psychologist*, vol. 64, no. 6, 2009, pp. 515–26, doi:10.1037/a0016755.

[59] Bresman, Henrik, and Todd R. Zenger. "The Impact of Diverse Work Experiences on the Development of Human Capital and Career Success." *Academy of Management Journal*, vol. 59, no. 2, 2016, pp. 469–93, doi:10.5465/amj.2014.0374.

[60] Amabile, Teresa M. "The Social Psychology of Creativity: A Componential Conceptualization." *Journal of Personality and Social Psychology*, vol. 45, no. 2, 1983, pp. 357–76, doi:10.1037/0022-3514.45.2.357.

Made in the USA
Monee, IL
02 August 2025